Family Power!

Family Power!

Mark E. Petersen

Bookcraft
Salt Lake City, Utah

Library of Congress Catalog Card Number: 80:68473
ISBN 0-88494-417-4

First Printing, 1981

Lithographed in the United States of America
PUBLISHERS PRESS
Salt Lake City, Utah

CONTENTS

THE ETERNAL UNIT

LOVE AT HOME

LEARNING THE GOSPEL

LAW AND OBEDIENCE

FATHER AND MOTHER

THE ARMOR OF RIGHTEOUSNESS

THE ETERNAL UNIT

FAMILY PLANNING

The expression "family planning" has different meaning to different people, and those differences vary as widely as personal opinions on marriage, size of families, and on the "new morality."

To some people, family planning means having no children. To others it means having one or two at most. This, of course, at times may promote the use of contraceptives and abortion.

To still others it means furnishing teen-agers with contraceptive devices with a total lack of instruction on chastity.

Family planning is all-important if we have the right definition for it. Of that we may be certain. But it must be good and it must be proper, which means but one thing: that it must be in full harmony with the divine word of God.

Without good family planning we could go like Rome, Greece and other early but well-advanced civilizations that discarded their high standards and fell into decay.

Good family life is vital to civilization.

Good family life cannot survive on relaxed moral standards.

Good family life disappears with increased abortions, marriageless unions and wide promiscuity.

Good family life ceases when people refuse to have children as God commanded them to do, but make of marriage a sensual convenience.

The destruction of good family life is a sheer violation of the laws of God, and is one of the worst forms of anti-Christ. Behavior which eliminates good family life is nothing short of suicidal.

God has provided for family planning, but it is His own kind, and the ways of God are not the ways of man. What is His kind? It is based firmly upon these principles:

1. Honorable marriage within the law, and temple marriage for faithful members of the Church.

2. Love at home. Honorable, clean and wholesome love, not the lust which the world now interprets as lovemaking. It must be love for God, genuine affection and complete fidelity between husband and wife, and a true devotion to children born to the home.

3. A willingness to have children. Did not the Almighty command us to multiply and replenish the earth? Has He ever rescinded that Law?

4. A willingness to seek first the kingdom of God and His righteousness. The home circle must be honorable, upright, and circumspect in obeying the commandments of the Lord Jesus Christ.

5. The establishment of a family routine in which gospel living becomes habitual, where children are taught the gospel from infancy, and then baptized at the proper age.

6. Paying due honor to the priesthood of God within the home.

7. Looking to the temple of the Lord as the gateway to seeking perfection, even as our Father which is in heaven is perfect.

8 Attendance at our authorized and regular Church services.

9. That we eschew all evil.

10. That we put on the whole armor of God.

Only this pattern for family planning can give true happiness.

THE GREATEST NEED

A family planner gave a lecture in which he told his audience that the two most important things in making a marriage succeed were love and common sense.

He made no mention at all of the greatest factor, which is spirituality.

As Latter-day Saints we look to the Lord for direction.

It was He who gave us the institution of marriage in the first place, and He who provides that family life is part of our exaltation in the world to come.

In fact, there can be no exaltation outside of the true family relationship. That is why we perform temple marriages. That is also why we teach that good home life on this earth is but a faint reflection of the eternal family life which once was ours in the presence of our Father, and which again we will experience eventually if we are faithful to the Lord.

Since family life is at the root of exaltation in the Kingdom of God, can it rest upon any foundation that excludes spirituality? Can individual members of a family reap all they should from their home life without spirituality?

Paul taught that the man is not without the woman, neither is the woman without the man in the Lord, and He further taught, in referring to our family line, that we without our relatives cannot be made perfect.

Love and common sense are most assuredly necessary in a happy marriage, but both in reality are products of true spirituality.

God is love. True love springs from Him, not from some mortal romance. Common sense is but a synonym for wisdom, and wisdom likewise is an attribute of God.

Then both love and common sense arise out of true spirituality, and good homes must rest upon all three.

Virtually every divorce has resulted from a violation of the commands of God by one party in the marriage or the other. Repentance and reformation, which are part of the spiritual development provided in the gospel, can heal every wound.

If couples will bring the gospel into the home and live the laws of God, including that which says we must do unto others as we would be done by, there would be little trouble in any marriage.

If regular family prayers were held, and meaningful home evenings were conducted, the spirit of God would be in the home, and there would be patience, forgiveness, love and harmony.

But it is all based on spirituality. Then can we exclude this vital factor from our marriage?

MAKING MARRIAGE WORK

In any association where two or more people are engaged, there is one great rule of successful relationships. It is the Golden Rule from the Savior's Sermon on the Mount.

If everyone would do to the other as they would be done by, all kinds of personal conflicts would be erased. It would put an end to selfishness, greed and avarice, which are the causes of quarrels, wars and crime.

Particularly is this rule good for a marriage and for the conduct of a home. "All things whatsoever ye would that men should do to you, do ye even so to them." (Matt. 7:12.)

Marriage should be forever. It should be based on the gospel of the Lord Jesus Christ, which should be lived and taught regularly in the home. This would assure success of home life, and would make it truly good.

But there are adverse elements too which enter some homes and which contribute to their breakdown. The monthly letter of the Royal Bank of Canada had something to say on that point, and we quote in part as follows:

"The approach young people make to marriage is a big feature about success in family building. There is a Hollywood jewelry store with a sign in the window: 'We Hire Out Wedding Rings.' A casual approach like that will seldom pay off in stability.

"Marriage is not something that is covered in a ceremony; it is not something in which success is assured if the young people have the same background, traditions and economic status. It is not guaranteed success by books, movie-made conceptions of married life, or anything else of a casual or superficial nature.

"The only thing that works effectively toward successful marriage is kinship of ideas and ideals. No blind faith in romantic love will serve, though this is a hard-to-erase social fiction."

Kinship of ideas and ideals can best be found through the gospel and the Church.

When Paul spoke to the Ephesians about "one Lord, one faith, [and] one baptism" (Eph. 4:5), he might have applied it to marriage as well, for successful marriage also requires the worship of the same God, the living of the same faith, and the acceptance of the same baptism, both of water and the Spirit.

God instituted marriage in the first place. It was for the establishment and preservation of family life, wherein parents live together in peace and harmony, wherein children are reared in the faith, and wherein the whole family may have an eye single to God and His work. "What God hath joined together, let no man put asunder" by evil deeds.

JUSTIFYING OURSELVES

The Lord will have no part in the so-called "justice" that we deal out to ourselves. He is the Judge and He sets the rules. Hypocrisy is no part of the divine nature.

And what are we talking about? Divorce. The breaking up of families. The injury done to innocent people, usually children.

There is a wave of divorce in America. There are too many divorces among Latter-day Saints. In almost every case, the wandering one justifies himself or herself, feels unappreciated, or unloved, or simply wants a change.

Divorces of couples who have been married for as many as thirty or forty years are becoming commonplace. It is appalling. And why? While some marital breakups may be justified, divorce often is a simple case of selfishness. The scriptures call it covetousness. And there is a law against that.

When the Savior was approached on the subject of divorce at one time, and reference was made to the divorces granted by Moses, He said: "For the hardness of your heart he wrote you this precept."

He made it clear that it was not so from the beginning, that God made male and female, ordained marriage and said "they twain shall be one flesh: so then they are no more twain, but one flesh." (Mark 10:4-9.)

And then He said: "What therefore God hath joined together, let no man put asunder." Is there no meaning to those words? Has God changed His mind?

He said that for this cause shall a man cleave to his wife. And what does *cleave* mean? Webster defines the word as: "to stick fast; to be faithful to; adhere."

The Lord used that same expression in modern revelation as He spoke of marriage. Said He:

"Thou shalt love thy wife with all thy heart, and shalt cleave unto her and none else." (D&C 42:22.)

Has that ceased to have a message? Is it not binding today, as well as any other revelation given to Joseph Smith?

Many men who seek divorce have roving eyes. Many of them have other feminine interests. There is nothing that makes a man lose his taste for his own wife as quickly as to have another woman in mind. The other woman, of course, is always "perfect"; she, like the king, can do no wrong. All the wrong is blamed on the unoffending wife. But the other woman, often beginning as only a friend, may become a husband-snatching robber.

Does not such a man realize that he is flying in the face of Almighty God and defying this revelation which tells him to love his wife, cleave to her and none else? Can he justify himself in such a sin?

To break up his home for another woman is tragic. But to break up two marriages — his own and hers — is worse. Can anyone, man or woman, justify that? It is robbery of the worst kind!

And what did the Lord say through Moses? "Thou shalt not covet." And especially did He say thou shalt not covet "anything that is thy neighbor's." And He mentioned the wife in particular. But it applies as well to the neighbor's husband. What is worse than husband snatching?

Wife stealing and husband stealing are sins in the eyes of God. The Lord requires that we preserve our marriages. Indeed they are intended to be forever.

We have the divine law plainly set forth. If we break it, there is only one viable answer and that is repentance. If a man has lost his love for his wife let him repent and woo her all over again. And let him shun other feminine interests like the plague.

We are under solemn covenant to serve God and keep His commandments. Among the most important covenants are those pertaining to marriage.

GOD'S WAYS — AND MAN'S

A mother and her five children went grocery shopping. Pushing their cart from aisle to aisle they all took part, apparently having a good time doing it.

Some wanted to buy one thing; others, something else, but

the list was in mother's hands and she kept everything under control.

But a disturbed bystander looked disdainfully at the children, and then assailed the mother with an intense verbal onslaught.

"What right do you have in this enlightened day to have so many children? Don't you know that a family should be limited to no more than two? What do you mean, having so many children?"

The mother, of course, was amazed, to say the least. She had no desire to debate with this angry stranger, so turning away, she entered another aisle and left her assailant behind.

But the incident started her on a serious line of thought. What if she had limited her family to two children? She looked at her two eldest. They were a boy and a girl. She was deeply grateful for them. But what of the other three?

There were Susan and Jerry, the twins. As she looked at them and contemplated their short five years in the family, her youngest child, Jenine took hold of her hand. Jenine was the most affectionate of them all.

If she were to do it all over again, knowing the children as she did, which of them would she have preferred to do without? The thought horrified her.

Had she stopped with only two children, Jenine, her loving little one, now but three years old, would never have graced their home. And neither would Jerry, a boy, every inch of him, and a good one. Could she ever think of being without Susan?

There was a complete bond of love and fellowship among those children. They made a happy family circle. Then she thought of her husband and herself, completing that circle. Would they wish to change it or reduce it if they could?

A good family is the highest expression of human life, more to be desired than riches, prestige, or anything else the world has to offer. And why?

Because it is the Lord's way. And did not the Psalmist say, "The Lord is righteous in all his ways"? (Ps. 145:17.)

But this bystander who assailed the little group in the grocery store, what of her point of view? It was "man's way" and reflected the philosophy of zero growth, completely contrary to the Lord's way.

No wonder Isaiah, speaking under inspiration, said, "neither are your ways my ways, saith the Lord." (Isa. 55:8.)

So there are the two philosophies: the Lord's and man's. We have a choice. Which way shall we go?

True Christians are under covenant to serve the Lord. Those covenants provide that we shall live by every word that proceeds from the mouth of God. (D&C 84:44.)

His divine word provides that we shall enter honorable marriage, that we have children, that we rear them in the faith and make every effort to save their souls.

We are to conduct our family life on the gospel plan. We bring the commandments — and the true gospel spirit — into our homes, living them and doing to each other as we would be done by.

When we live the gospel in the home we exclude the contentions that arise in some families, as well as selfishness, cruelty, wrongful indulgence, and vulgarity.

And as we live the gospel we bring into our homes the influence of the Holy Spirit, including love, harmony, patience, consideration and true worship that helps us to become like our Father in Heaven.

Living the Christlike life within our home circle makes for the highest level of human existence.

THE FATHER'S ROLE

The Lord did not intend that there should be bachelors and "old maids." He provided that all should engage in the married state.

His purpose is clearly indicated in His gospel teachings. It is

intended that all of His children have opportunity to become
"perfect as your Father which is in Heaven is perfect."

To become like God is our greatest aim. Our lives should be
constantly planned to achieve this great destiny. But proper
marriage is essential to it.

We are the children of God — we belong to His eternal
family. Family life is basic to progress in the gospel. There can be
no family life without marriage.

As part of our progress toward becoming like our Heavenly
Father, the Lord provided us with temple marriage, wherein the
bonds of matrimony survive death and the resurrection. As Paul
said, man is not without the woman, neither is the woman
without the man in the Lord.

Temple marriage provides also for the preservation of family ties to children, to grandchildren and subsequent generations. Elijah came to turn the hearts of the fathers to their
children and the children to their fathers. Without eternal family
ties there is no exaltation in the presence of God.

It was with this in mind that President Joseph F. Smith said:
"We believe that every man holding the holy Priesthood should
be married, with the very few exceptions of those who through
infirmities of mind or body are not fit for marriage. . . . We hold
that no man who is marriageable is fully living his religion who
remains unmarried. He is doing a wrong to himself by retarding
his progress, by narrowing his experiences, and to society by the
undesirable example that he sets to others. . . .

"We say to our young people, get married and marry aright.
Marry in the faith, and let the ceremony be performed in the
place God has appointed. Live so that you may be worthy of this
blessing."

Then the President added: "The command which God gave
in the beginning to multiply and replenish the earth is still in
force upon the children of men. Possibly no greater sin could be
committed by the people who have embraced this gospel than to
prevent or to destroy life." (Joseph F. Smith, *Gospel Doctrine* [Salt
Lake City: Deseret Book Co., 1966], page 275.)

The role of man then is to marry and marry well; marry in the temples of God, and live to be worthy of such marriage. It is also to be loving and kind to the wife so taken in the holy covenant.

Husband and wife are required by the Lord to have children in righteousness, and then to rear them in the light of the gospel so that those children may believe in God, keep his commandments, and in turn receive their eternal salvation.

Fathers and mothers must be partners in this holy assignment given them of the Lord. To refuse is to violate some of the greatest laws that God has given us.

TEMPLES ARE GATEWAYS

Family planning must always include taking our dear ones to the temples of the Lord.

Exaltation comes to us on a family basis and not as single individuals. Since temple ordinances are required for exaltation in the kingdom of God, and since we are to be exalted as families, then our families need the temple blessings. Hence the importance of making the necessary effort to provide them.

It was Paul who taught that the man is not without the woman, nor the woman without the man in the Lord. (1 Cor. 11:11.)

But our children are part of that family circle too, and they must likewise receive what the temple has to offer. That is what makes our families eternal, surviving both death and resurrection. Hence the temple becomes a grand gateway to the celestial kingdom.

There are two parts to the gospel, over all. One has to do with living the good life. The other is compliance with the required ordinances of the gospel.

All gospel ordinances relate to the celestial kingdom. This includes baptism, pointing to the need of baptism as a saving ordinance. The Savior said it is required to fulfill all righteousness. That is why he was baptized.

As we have these two general areas within the gospel, so we have two kinds of gospel ordinances: those which are given only in the temple, and those which are given outside of the temple. Both are required by the Lord.

Many do not consider the temple blessings as saving ordinances, and therefore they do not seek them. But temple ordinances are as essential as baptism, and without baptism, the Lord said, we cannot even see the kingdom of heaven.

Then will we not make the necessary effort to take our families to the temple and there receive these blessings?

President Spencer W. Kimball has suggested that in each home we display a picture of a temple, either of the Salt Lake Temple, or of the one serving the district in which we live, or of any other one of the Lord's holy houses.

This is a teaching suggestion. As we daily see the picture of the temple, it will remind us of the importance of the ordinances given in that house. It will be an inspiration to all to live to be worthy of admittance. It will remind us of the essential nature of the ordinances of the gospel.

One of the most important lessons is that it will be a constant reminder to the young people to look to the day when they may go to the temple themselves, either to perform vicarious baptisms for the dead, or to prepare to go on missions, or very importantly, to be married.

To be married in the temple must be one of our major goals in life. Temple marriage is a *saving ordinance* of the Church, as much so as baptism. It is more than a marriage, such as civil marriage. It is a sacred ordinance leading to the eternal destiny of families.

So temples are gateways to eternal happiness. They open the way to exaltation in the presence of the Lord.

A GREAT RESPONSIBILITY

The Prophet Joseph Smith taught that performance of temple work on behalf of our dead is one of our greatest responsibilities. The work to which he referred was work for our own particular dead, our own deceased relatives, for generations back.

It is not enough to merely "go to the temple." We must go to the temple to save our own dead ancestry. This cannot be done without genealogical research by which we identify those dead, so that we can not only perform baptisms for them, but likewise the higher ordinances including the sealing of their immediate families as we have ours sealed there, and then the sealing of our previous generations.

Each child has parents to whom he must be sealed. Each parent has a family to be sealed. This cannot be accomplished unless the generations are bound together, each child to his own parents, each parent to his own husband or wife and they to their own offspring. This necessitates going from generation to generation.

Speaking of the importance of doing this work, President Joseph Fielding Smith wrote in *Seeking After Your Dead*, page 35, as follows:

"It matters not what else we may have been called to do, or what position we occupy, or how faithfully in other ways we have labored in the Church, none are exempt from the great obligation of performance of temple work for the dead.

"It is required of the apostle as well as of the humblest elder. Place, or distinction, or long service in the Church, in the mission fields, the stakes of Zion, or where or how else it may have been, will not entitle one to disregard the salvation of one's dead.

"Some may feel that if they pay their tithing, attend to their regular meetings, and other duties, give of their substance to feed the poor, perchance spend one or two years preaching in the world, that they are absolved from further duty.

"But the greatest and grandest duty of all is to labor for the dead. We may and should do all these other things, for which reward will be given, but if we neglect the weightier privilege and commandment, notwithstanding all our other good works, we shall find ourselves under severe condemnation."

The Prophet Joseph spoke of the Saints becoming saviors on Mt. Zion, and then he added:

"But how are they to become saviors on Mt. Zion? By building their temples, erecting their baptismal fonts, and going forth and receiving all the ordinances, baptisms, confirmations, washings, anointings, ordinations, and sealing powers upon their heads in behalf of all their progenitors who are dead." (*Teachings of the Prophet Joseph Smith*, comp. Joseph Fielding Smith [Salt Lake City: Deseret Book Co., 1938], page 330.)

But how can we do this unless we know who our progenitors are? Hence the vital necessity of each of us doing our genealogical research so that we may identify our dead ancestry, and then do the work for them in the temples of the Lord.

GOING TO THE TEMPLE

President Heber J. Grant was a powerful advocate of temple work. Not only did he attend the temple regularly throughout his life, but even while he was carrying the burden of presidency he still set a great example.

At one time he said:

"I am a thorough convert to the fact that if we make up our minds to take the time, there is hardly any person who cannot find the time to go through the temple once or twice a week, no matter how busy he may be or how many duties devolve upon him.

"I wish to ask the saints to try and shape their affairs so that they can occasionally go to the temple.

"I am anxious to encourage the people to press on in securing their genealogies, and after doing so, to labor in our temples. I am sure that for each and every one of you who has determination the Lord will open the way whereby you can accomplish the labor.

"To my mind, one of the great privileges that we as Latter-day Saints enjoy is that of doing temple work for those of our ancestors who have died without a knowledge of the gospel. I believe that if a person has a desire to do temple work he can find a way to do it. The important thing is the desire. I do not ask anybody who is as busy as I am to go to the temple any more often than I go.

"I had felt for years that I did not have time to go to the temple, but finally I got the desire to go, and from that time on I have had no difficulty in finding time to go once a week. Occasionally I go twice a week.

"I believe that if I can find time to go to the temple and to do temple work once a week, there is hardly a man in the entire Church of Jesus Christ of Latter-day Saints but who can find the same time if he wishes to plan his work accordingly. I am speaking of people who live where there is a temple, in Manti, Logan, and elsewhere. If we cannot go to the temple ourselves we can hire somebody else to go.

"If you get it into your heart and soul that this is one of the most important things you as Latter-day Saints can do, you will find a way to do it."

WE BUILD TEMPLES

The Latter-day Saints are a distinctive people in many respects. One of their most remarkable characteristics is that they are temple builders. In the accepted biblical sense, no other people on earth build temples to the Lord.

These temples are not merely beautiful structures. They are

houses of the Lord. But they are not alone houses of the Lord in which the Almighty might visit the earth. They are places in which the work of the Lord is done. That is what makes them houses of the Lord.

And what is this work of the Lord?

It is the performance of saving ordinances, without which there is no exaltation in His presence.

The Savior commanded us to become perfect, even as our Father in heaven is perfect (Matt. 5:48). Paul explained to the Ephesians that this perfection comes through the organization of his Church (Eph. 4:11-14).

In all ages of the world the Lord has commanded His people to build temples. Even while the ancient Israelites were traveling in the wilderness they carried with them the portable tabernacle which under their circumstances served the purpose. But it did have a purpose — an important and sacred one.

The Nephites were commanded to build temples, again for a sacred purpose. And when the Prophet Joseph Smith was raised up as the great restorer of latter days, the Lord commanded him to build temples. The Saints responded even in their extreme poverty, as well as under severe persecution.

When they came to Utah, the Saints could hardly wait to build more temples. One of President Brigham Young's first acts in Salt Lake Valley was to designate the place for a temple, and while that one was under construction, others were built in Logan, St. George and Manti. But why this urgency?

Because the Saints knew that certain essential saving ordinances were available only in a temple, and they so loved the gospel that they wished to receive all of its ordinances as soon as possible.

When the Prophet Joseph instructed the people of his day to erect the Nauvoo temple he said:

"As soon as the temple and baptismal font are prepared we calculate to give the elders of Israel their washings and anointings and attend to those last and more impressive ordinances *without which we cannot obtain celestial thrones."* (*Teachings*, page 362.)

That is why we build temples. These essential ordinances are required for both the living and the dead. Without them none can receive their celestial thrones.

Latter-day Saints then have two responsibilities regarding the temples: One is to receive in them their own essential ordinances, and the other is to perform identical ones for their dead ancestors.

UPSURGE IN MARRIAGE

A short time ago United Press International news service published a report from Washington indicating that during the 1970s the number of unmarried persons in the United States living together not only doubled, but reached a total of two million.

As part of this report, the service indicated that the divorce rate in America is the highest in the world.

Of the two million living together without marriage, the report said that in 1,212,000 cases, the women moved in with the men, and in 702,000 instances the men moved in with the women.

Frightening as all this is, and demoralizing as is its effect, there is a ray of hope from another source. In spite of the trend toward "living together," now more and more couples, both young and old, are entering matrimony, and an increasing number of their weddings is being performed by the clergy in denominational churches.

Helen Johnson, editor of *Bride's Magazine*, comments on this trend and says: "The 'Me Decade' is nearly over, and now people want that wonderful hopeful and happy state that marriage provides. They've found the need for a network of support that a family offers."

In 1980 *Bride's* conducted a poll among its readers and discovered some interesting results. Of two thousand women who responded, 98 percent said they wanted formal weddings complete with gowns, trains and veils, bridesmaids and maids of honor, and a large, traditional wedding reception. On top of that, a full 99 percent said they wanted to get married in a religious ceremony.

"People want to share their lives with other people," Johnson says. "Marriage is a source of emotional nourishment and pleasure. Young people want it. Older people want it again. People who have been married and divorced before are giving marriage and themselves a second chance. It represents a fresh start in life."

Judy Cantor, license supervisor in Reno, Nevada, is quoted as saying that the main reason women now want a real marriage is peace of mind. "I think any woman still wants to get married. It is one of the most rewarding and fulfilling things a person can do," she said.

We have it repeated to us frequently that civilization itself rests upon good family life, and there can be no good family life without honorable marriage.

For Latter-day Saints, of course, temple marriage is the goal. It is part and parcel of their religion. It is not only for eternity, but it provides great blessings in this life also. The ratio of divorces among persons married in the temple is still but a mere fraction of those of the public at large.

STRONGER FAMILIES

Family life is now being recognized around the globe, not only as the basic unit of civilized society but as a growing power in stabilizing the present shaky conditions in the world.

Newspapers from Australia to Finland editorialize on this trend. Magazines repeatedly produce articles defending the family as the ideal institution for human living.

One of Australia's leading newspapers recently editorialized on the women's liberation movement and called attention to the fact that any movement which tends to weaken the family as an institution is opposed to the common good. Any movement which tends to preserve the family contributes to the common good.

The editors of *The Australian* wrote: "A family may not be the most efficient unit from an accountant's point of view, a lawyer's point of view or a sociologist's point of view. Not everybody has a family. Not every family is happy. But, taken overall, the family is the most powerful influence for good in all society. For every family that is divided, unhappy or at odds within itself, there are a hundred families where there is love and trust and communal discipline and interdependence and unqualified mutual support, held together by bonds which no laws can create — but which laws can break or damage.

"Laws, however well-meant, which can weaken family ties, which encourage young people to go first to the State instead of to the family, are laws which will weaken the very fabric of society. Legislation arising from this report, or from any other source, should be measured against this criterion. If it does not measure up, it should not be passed."

The *Family Circle* magazine, widely distributed through grocery stores, has carried repeated articles defending the family, and branding as a myth the reports that family life is on the way out.

For example, Earl C. Gottschalk, Jr., writing in the December 13, 1977, issue of that magazine, said that claims indicating the family is a dying institution "are all false." He quotes surveys made by college research teams at University of Southern California and other schools.

One survey showed that more than half of the 205,000 students contacted in one sampling said that raising a family was one of their most important objectives in life, ahead of financial or business values.

Two thousand Los Angeles families were sampled, showing the vast majority reported warm and highly satisfactory family relationships. A study at the University of Minnesota showed that the majority of young people had happy relationships with their parents.

Family life was instituted by the Almighty. If it is properly conducted it can and will produce the greatest satisfaction in life. But one of the basic rules for its success is the old and established rule given by the Savior in the Sermon on the Mount:

"All things whatsoever ye would that men should do to you, do ye even so to them." (Matt. 7:12.)

THE PLACE OF FAMILY

Apart from family life, the human race has no future, only the emptiness of solitary space and the dance of death. It is the destiny of flesh and blood to be familial.

Such is the statement of Michael Novak in an article in *Harper's Magazine,* condensed by *Reader's Digest.*

He then continued:

"Clearly, the family is the critical center of social force. It is a seedbed of economic skills and attitudes toward work. It is a stronger agency of educational success than the school and a stronger teacher of the religious imagination than the church. Political and social planning in a wise social order begins with the axiom: *What strengthens the family strengthens society.*

"Even when poverty and disorientation strike, as over the generations they so often do, it is family strength that most defends individuals against alienation, lassitude or despair. The world around the family is fundamentally unjust.

"The state and its agents, and the economic system and its agencies, are never fully to be trusted. One unforgettable law has been learned through all the disasters and injustices of the last thousand years: *If things go well with the family, life is worth living; when the family falters, life falls apart.*"

With all their meanderings, people are steadily beginning to waken to this great fact: That life as we know it — successful life — rests upon the strength of the family association.

THE POWER OF FAMILIES

There are elements that seek to break down the system of family life that has characterized civilization from time immemorial, and seek to abolish the institution of marriage in its entirety.

It is, therefore, refreshing to note support for the family and for proper marriage as it comes from sources of great strength in the world.

Recently the monthly letter of the Royal Bank of Canada had this to say about the value of family life:

"The family holds its pre-eminent place in our way of life because it is the only possible base upon which a society of responsible human beings has ever found it practicable to build for the future and maintain the values they cherish in the present.

"The successful family is not one in which there is no conflict, but one in which the husband and wife use their resources of common sense and ingenuity to work out the sharing of responsibility and practice give-and-take.

"If the family were to be swept away, the world would become a place of regimentation, chaos and desolation. Why? Because the family fulfills at least three vital functions: it provides sustenance and trains its members in the art of surviving; it provides the earliest group association, teaching the art of social living; and it is the primary place where the values and knowledge of culture are passed from generation to generation.

"That is only a small part of the service given by the family to individual members of it. There are other functions. The family is closely related to social change. Ideas must develop there before the community adopts them.

"From birth to death, there is scarcely an action that can be performed by a person that is not guided and colored by what is learned in the family. Bitterness within the family works its way out into society. The person who is frustrated in family life is likely to become the cynic of world life.

"But wholesome and constructive thinking in the family will penetrate all society. The person who learns within the family to accommodate to others, to subordinate, when necessary, personal interest to the interest of the group, and to tolerate in others' fads and habits he would condemn in himself — that person has learned many of the lessons necessary to becoming a good worker, a good leader and a good citizen."

LOVE AT HOME

"WITH ALL THY HEART..."

There are two commandments in the scriptures in which the Lord commands that we love with all our hearts.

It is a singular thing that one relates to our allegiance to God, and the other to our wife or husband.

The first and great commandment teaches us to love the Lord our God with all our hearts, might, mind and strength. This of necessity must be the first and greatest of them all.

There would be no basis for faith or trust in God if we did not love Him. But neither is there any basis for true advancement in His kingdom if we are half-hearted in our attitude toward Him.

We must love Him with all our heart, with all our might, mind and strength. Half-hearted measures bring no reward. On the other hand, we are plainly told that if we receive the commandments with a doubtful heart and keep them with slothfulness, we are damned. (D&C 58:26-29.)

The Doctrine and Covenants (section 4) teaches us that the Lord interprets this love in terms of service, for He says that we are to serve Him with all our heart, might, mind and strength. Devoted service to Him brings the blessings of eternity. Nothing else will.

But there is that other law: "Thou shalt love thy wife with all thy heart, and shalt cleave unto her and none else." (D&C 42:22.)

That is an all-encompassing principle with respect to success in marriage. We are commanded in the first place to love our wife and to do so without reservation, with all our heart.

With many couples, love wanes and is lost. What is the answer to such a condition; divorce? If a person robbed a bank, what would be the cure for that — to rob another bank?

With every one of the commands of God there is the law of repentance. If we disobey the command, we must repent, make necessary adjustments, and never repeat the sin.

In the case of a man losing his love for his wife, what is he to do? Isn't repentance the answer once again?

Was there ever a divorce in which the laws of God were not broken by one or both of the parties?

The gospel is a law of love, forgiveness, patience, understanding, kindness, and even turning the other cheek. It is going the extra mile. It is living the Golden Rule and doing to others as we would be done by.

If the Golden Rule were lived in every family, and husbands and wives treated each other as they themselves would like to be treated, would there ever be a divorce?

It is when selfishness, greed, or lust enters in that marriages suffer. These elements form the basis of family quarrels, too. The Lord commands against family quarrels, and all quarrels for that matter. Did He not tell the Nephites when He was among them that the spirit of disputation is the spirit of the devil? Then if we quarrel do we not do so by the spirit of the devil? (3 Ne. 11:29.)

The command is first to love our wives. Then it is to "cleave" unto them, which is to stay by them. To cleave unto them allows no room for breaking up a marriage.

And next the law says "and none else." That is, we are to love our own wife and none else. There is no place in a Latter-day Saint marriage for a "triangle."

These laws apply equally to wives and husbands. Wives are to love their husbands with all their hearts, and cleave unto them, and none else.

The gospel is the answer to all our troubles, and it is especially so with regard to marriage and love at home.

STRONG HOME TIES

Both apostles Paul and Peter wrote about the last days and indicated that perilous times would characterize them, that natural affection would be lost, and that various evil designs would dominate the minds and acts of men.

Those times are here now. The best defense against their influence is the home, and the best defense of the home is to be found in strong and righteous parents.

The Lord has given priesthood holders the presidency within their own homes — in righteousness. In many instances fathers fail in this responsibility, and then of course mothers must assume the leadership role — also in righteousness. Many of them do, and raise wonderful families. Some do not.

But to the man of the house is given the first call to lead the family from the evils of the day into realms of cleanliness and faith. How shall he do it?

Bringing the gospel into the home so that each member of the family learns it and lives it is the only path of safety. Becoming Christlike is the ultimate aim of every right-thinking person, and that can be achieved only in living the gospel.

Love must prevail in the home in order to achieve it. The spirit of God is the spirit of love. God is love, say the scriptures. To become like Him we ourselves must personify love and extend it to all members of the family.

Men are told in scripture to love their wives with all their hearts and to cleave to them and to none else. This is a basic law of proper marriage and good home life. The principle applies likewise to wives.

The Golden Rule stands next to it: Each man and wife should do to the other as they would be done by. Each parent and child should follow the same pattern. If this were done, selfishness would be eliminated from the home and with it family quarrels, pro-divorce situations, and dishonesty. The spirit of love, which is the spirit of Christ, would then prevail.

Who can best promote such a situation in the home? The leaders, of course. And who are the leaders? Father and mother. Peace and love in the household must begin with them. It likewise will end with them if they permit it.

Father should take his place at the head of the house and as the priesthood holder should so exercise his priestly position in righteousness that gospel principles will be taught, gospel living will be exemplified, and Christlike traits of character will be developed within the entire family group.

Fathers who fail to teach the gospel to their children and who do not set proper examples are recreant to their high calling and will be held accountable for such failures before God.

Husbands who fail to "love their wives with all their hearts, and cleave unto them and none else" contribute to the breakdown of home life and can be hazards to an entire community.

In this evil day, fathers and mothers must take upon themselves the "whole armor of God," as Paul expressed it, and make home building their first and major project in life, for as President David O. McKay said, no other success can compensate for failure in that sacred circle.

LOVE AT HOME

A wise man once said: "The most important thing a father can do for his children is to love their mother."

This recalls the expression of President David O. McKay: "No other success in life can compensate for failure in the home."

Success or failure in the home rests in large measure in the hands of the father. Any man possibly can wreck his family life. And yet there are many instances where the mother has been sufficiently strong and faithful to rear her brood properly in spite of the evil examples of a father.

The converse is likewise true. Many a man has made a supreme effort in rearing his family in the absence of the good influence of a mother. But there are more errant fathers than there are misdirected mothers!

To be truly strong, homes need the combined effort of both father and mother working together, planning unitedly for their children, and teaching them in a spirit of true harmony.

That is why the Lord stressed fidelity between husband and wife. That is why He commanded the father to "love thy wife with all thy heart, and shalt cleave unto her and none else." (D&C 42:22.)

That is why love and love alone can make a family good — love for each other, love for God and love for righteousness.

When father sets the example, the rest of the family is likely to follow. So what can he best do for his little ones? Love their mother and cooperate fully with her in rearing the family.

Where love is missing, the cooperation will be missing also. So without that love, the father bequeaths only difficulty to his own flesh and blood.

OUR TOGETHERNESS

Family life is the most wholesome form of living known to man. It builds individuals, it builds communities and it makes the world strong. No nation is stronger than its families.

But in family life we must build the concept of togetherness — that we belong to each other.

Many of our Church families are known as "strong" families. Wherever they live, separated as they often are, such family members are known for their fine character, their dependability and their loyalty to Church and country.

Some families fight. Children fight, often following the example of parents. When parents recognize the need of togetherness and build that concept into their marriage, they likewise build it into the minds of their children, who learn to appreciate each other instead of thinking otherwise of a brother or sister.

Lilian G. Katz, writing in *Parents'* magazine gives good advice on this subject and, among other things, said in a recent column:

"Finally, if your chidren say genuinely nasty things to you about one another, use those occasions to indicate that you do not agree, and to explain that even though we get angry at each other, we still belong to each other.

"When we consistently remind children of their unalterable belonging to us and to each other, we strengthen their sense of safety; which is perhaps a prerequisite for the development of the capacity for brotherly and sisterly love."

FAMILY SOLIDARITY

A strong plea for family harmony is made by President Spencer W. Kimball in a book published by the Deseret Book Company.

The volume, entitled *Marriage and Divorce,* provides direct and persuasive reading which will benefit every Latter-day Saint. It is based on an address given by the President before a packed BYU audience in the Marriott Center.

Expressing great concern about the stability of marriage, and more particularly among the younger couples, he said:

". . . Things worry us considerably because there are too many divorces, and they are increasing. It has come to be a common thing to talk about divorce. The minute there is a little crisis or a little argument in the family, we talk about divorce and we rush to see an attorney. This is not the way of the Lord. We should go back and adjust our problems and make our marriage compatible and sweet and blessed."

President Kimball gave a simple "never-failing formula that will guarantee to every couple a happy and eternal marriage.

"First, there must be the proper approach toward marriage, which contemplates the selection of a spouse who reaches as nearly as possible the pinnacle of perfection in all the matters that are of importance to the individuals. Then those two parties must come to the altar in the temple realizing that they must work hard toward this successful joint living.

"Second, there must be great unselfishness, forgetting self and directing all of the family life and all pertaining thereunto to the good of the family, and subjugating self.

"Third, there must be continued courting and expressions of affection, kindness, and consideration to keep love alive and growing.

"Fourth, there must be complete living of the commandments of the Lord as defined in the gospel of Jesus Christ."

As President Kimball said, "the formula is simple; the ingredients are few, though there are many amplifications of each. But the marriage depends first and always on the two spouses, who can always make their marriage successful and happy if they are determined, unselfish, and righteous.

"With these ingredients properly mixed and continually kept functioning, it is quite impossible for unhappiness to come, for misunderstandings to continue, or for breaks to occur. Divorce attorneys would need to transfer to other fields and divorce courts would be padlocked.

"Love cannot be expected to last forever unless it is continually fed with portions of love, and manifestations of esteem and admiration, the expressions of gratitude, and the consideration of unselfishness.

"Marriage is not a legal coverall. Rather, it means sacrifice, sharing, and even a reduction of some personal liberties. It means children who bring with them financial burdens, service burdens, care and worry burdens, but also it means the deepest and sweetest emotions of all.

"Some think of happiness as a glamorous life of ease, luxury, and constant thrills; but true marriage is based on a happiness that is more than that, one that comes from giving, serving, sharing, sacrificing and selflessness."

FAMILY TRIANGLES

Jealousy has no place in the family circle. But too often, it is there.

The "triangle," usually thought of in connection with threats to the family, is related to a third party outside of the home. But there is jealousy, too, within the sacred circle itself.

Sometimes fathers or mothers will become jealous of their own child when that little one tends to give more attention to one parent than to the other.

"Mama's boy" or "Daddy's girl" can be the root of it. Normally, of course, boys and their fathers grow a little more congenial, just as do daughters and their mothers. They have more in common, and that seems naturally to create a close companionship which should not be objectionable to anyone.

But when a little girl, tired of mother's corrections all day long, seems overpleased to see daddy returning from work, and gives him an especial ray of sunshine, mother may become jealous.

Fathers have developed similar adverse feelings when a boy relates better to the mother who provides most of the parental time in rearing the boy, because often the father is away from home so much that a warm companionship is not created.

Parents should recognize any such signs of difficulty, and erase them while they are yet in the formative stage. In true love there is no room for conflict.

BATTERED FAMILIES

The above headline was also the caption for an article in the *U.S. News and World Report*, in which that magazine surveyed the troubled families of America.

It said: "So widespread is the problem of family violence — abuse in some form occurs in more than half of all U.S. households — that some analysts are calling it a national nightmare."

The article estimated that fifty million Americans fall victim every year to some form of physical harm inflicted by another family member.

Quoting the National Institute of Mental Health, it said that 16 percent of all married people are physically attacked by husband or wife each year and eight million children are victims of physical assault by their parents.

Such assault is not to be interpreted in terms of the discipline Solomon advocated when he said "spare the rod and spoil the child."

This is physical abuse — severe beatings — which send thousands to hospitals for medical care, and other thousands to the morgue.

This report comes on the heels of efforts by certain groups to destroy our system of family life, to break down marriage and otherwise lead us to the Russian plan of destroying the home and rearing children by the state.

It is the breakdown of family life that causes all of this abuse. It is the family quarrel that leads to assault and battery and sometimes even murder.

It is the loss of filial love and understanding that sends battered children to hospitals by tens of thousands and five thousand a year to their death.

What further evidence do sensible people need to realize that we must come back to good family life, and quickly?

Love at home is the great need of today; love between

husband and wife, and between parents and children. That in turn would solve many of our juvenile problems of today.

Americans need to wake up to the jeopardy we are in.

Breakdown of love at home will bring a collapse of the family itself, and when the family goes, so goes the nation. No country can endure without good citizenship, and that kind of citizenship comes only from stable homes.

Family solidarity is rooted in the gospel of the Lord Jesus Christ. Isn't it time for our so-called Christian nations to start living His teachings?

What would — or wouldn't — national observance of the Golden Rule do for this or any other nation!

THAT GOLDEN RULE

If peace ever returns to the world, it must be through the principle of the Golden Rule. There can be no peace until mankind adopts the principle of doing to others as each would be done by.

The Savior taught us that the second great commandment is to love our neighbor as ourselves. When this is done, of course peace reigns, there is good will on all sides, and only a desire to be kind and thoughtful and helpful in every heart.

But how is that law implemented? It is by the adoption of the Golden Rule, which is the very essence of the second commandment.

"All things whatsoever ye would that men should do to you, do ye even so to them." (Matt. 7:12.)

This law can work wonders in every phase of life, if only it is used. Think for a moment of the family as an example. Would there ever be a family quarrel if this law were observed by all members? Would not each one endeavor to please the other in the best way possible? Would it not engender "love at home" as nothing else could?

This law could banish divorce. It could abolish selfishness, conflicts, vengeful tactics, and bitterness. It could establish harmony, good will and genuine affection.

Isn't this the true Spirit of Christ? Isn't that what the Christmas message was about — peace on earth, good will toward men? And shouldn't that Spirit be with us all year around?

But not only does this law work well at home. It is effective in every walk in life; in our employment, our recreation, our school activities — in all things! Live the Golden Rule and see how it works!

THE PURE IN HEART

If we must be pure in heart to see God, as the scriptures say, how many people today will qualify?

For us, His people, the Lord has commanded: "Be ye clean that bear the vessels of the Lord." He also has said, "Behold the Lord requireth the heart and a willing mind," and added, "Let all things be done in cleanliness." (D&C 38:42; 64:34; 42:41.)

He has told us that He cannot look upon sin with the least degree of allowance. And why? What makes Him so strict with regard to obedience to His commandments?

Always we must remember that He commands us to be perfect as He is. (Matt. 5:48). That is our destiny. Paul told the Ephesians that we must achieve the perfection of the Savior, even to the "measure of the stature of the fulness of Christ." (Eph. 4:12-13.)

The Lord could not be other than strict with us, for how can anyone achieve perfection by imperfect means?

A clean mind and a pure heart have always been the standard of acceptance with the Lord. He is pure and He is clean. To become like Him, can we be otherwise?

Unclean minds are responsible for most of the distress in the world. They produce all the pornography, from styles and books to movies. They must be blamed for the rampant perversions and promiscuity and for the epidemic of diseases that immorality foists upon an unsuspecting public.

What a sad reflection it is when a film denounced by the police as obscene suddenly draws such large crowds that the theater owners say they "never had it so good!"

Every form of crime and corruption emanates from a filthy brain. So do the alcohol, tobacco, and drug addictions, and with them the thousands of highway deaths chalked up to tipsy drivers.

In some circles the unclean begins to take on an air of respectability with the assertion that sin is no longer bad. With all such it becomes a lifestyle to wallow in filth.

One of the worst results of the public emphasis on pornography is the infiltration of certain perversions into family life, when some husbands and wives indulge in practices hitherto found only in brothels. They seem to think that anything goes within the home, which is the worst kind of delusion.

When will we come to our senses and realize that only through cleanliness and goodness can the race survive? The unclean is of the devil! Filth is worse than common dirt! It is more like rotting food or open sewage, spreading disease and more corruption.

If the world chooses to walk the filthy path, it has its free agency, but for followers of Christ there can be no way but the clean way. Filthy living is SIN in capital letters.

SUCCESS AT HOME

The Royal Bank of Canada produces a monthly letter which is one of the best in the business. It deals with sound character as a fundamental element in good business.

In one issue it discussed the Golden Rule and showed how that principle can bring prosperity to business. But it also showed how essential it is in family life and in group and community relationships.

It began with this paragraph:

"The Golden Rule ranks in history with the great pronouncements on the rights of man. It is also the distinguishing badge of ethical business. It says in one sentence the whole substance of the teaching of the law and the prophets on conduct between individuals and groups."

In the final analysis, good human relations are a reflection of family behavior. "As the twig is bent . . ."; "as the child is reared . . ."; the "child is the father to the man," etc.

If the Golden Rule were lived in every family its influence would be felt throughout the world. But when it is ignored in the family, where can it be found elsewhere?

The Golden Rule is the key to peace.

Home is the place where it can best be taught and lived.

Then what shall the family do? It should become Christian enough to live this most glorious rule of harmony and happiness. It should put selfishness aside and begin truly to do to others as each would be done by.

The Savior taught this rule in many ways. He told the Nephites to stop quarrelling, impressing upon them the great fact that people quarrel only by the spirit of the devil, never by the spirit of God (3 Ne. 11).

What if there were no more family quarrels?

And He taught people to stop being selfish, never to covet, never to steal or otherwise be dishonest.

Mercy was His watchword, forgiveness His standard. Reconciliation was laid down as a rule of life; revenge is to be forever shunned.

The Sermon on the Mount and the Ten Commandments are filled with expressions of the Golden Rule. Why do we not live them, if we are so interested in achieving peace and happiness?

Since patterns of conduct are formed in the home — even in

the cradle — shouldn't Christian ideals become standard in all families? Should we not cast out all semblance of un-Christian-like conduct?

Should we not begin to live the gospel effectively in the home?

TO TOUCH BASE IS GOOD

Each one of us would be greatly blessed if he or she would daily "touch base with Jesus Christ."

In the whole structure of our lives, He should be the chief cornerstone.

And how may we daily keep in touch with Him?

One way is through daily prayer, of course. Another is the daily reading of a verse of scripture about Christ from one of the four gospels or Third Nephi. Such reading, as is the case with earnest prayer, can provide for us a sweet spirit that will last the day through.

But another effective way of "touching base" with Him is to do at least one good turn daily.

He gave us the Golden Rule which is to treat others as we would be done by. Have we ever tried to live that law — really — for a full day at a time? Have we stopped to think, before each deed involving other people, what it would be like to be on the other side of the transaction?

If each time we deal with other people we would stop and consider the Golden Rule, our lives would change materially.

The Lord said that if we love Him we are to keep His commandments. If we fail to honor the Golden Rule, do we honor Him, or keep His commandments? With each attempt to love our neighbor as ourselves, we draw nearer to Him and more like Him.

That is the happy way of life. That is really "touching base."

LEARNING THE GOSPEL

HOME AS A TARGET

The Church of Jesus Christ of Latter-day Saints is certainly to be congratulated on its consistent effort to teach good family life. Its program to protect and bolster the home is one of its most important objectives.

Such also should be the goal of every state and nation, for without good homes, civilization itself can die.

Seemingly, much opposition to the establishment and perpetuation of these good homes comes from pro-abortion forces and from the effort to place women in the national work force, putting even young girls into military positions, on highway construction jobs, and hiring them to drive dump trucks. It seems that anything goes to "emancipate" women.

Mixing women and men in athletic events, and in locker rooms, helps to break down womanhood, and for that matter, true manhood, also. There is little honor where there is no mutual respect as between men and women.

But there are other dangers. A recent issue of *Time* magazine quotes Murray A. Strauss, sociologist, as saying that every year eight million Americans are assaulted by other members of their own families.

He said that sixteen out of every hundred families have violent fights each year, many ending in severe beatings and sometimes murder. He said that more than a third of all brothers and sisters violently fight each other.

The million-a-year youngsters who run away from home to escape the vicious tempers of their parents, or to get away from incest and other abuse, represent one of the most frightening aspects of the whole picture.

What is the cause of it all? What is the answer?

One major reason for the difficulty is the immaturity of many parents who actually have never really "grown up," who give way to temper tantrums, or indulge in extreme selfishness. They simply do not know how to be parents.

Lack of religion in the home is another serious fault, for gospel living is the best deterrent to evil that any home can have.

Certainly parents must learn how to be parents, and learn that rearing children is their great responsibility. Parents must learn the meaning of family loyalty. Togetherness which was discussed so much a few years ago must now become a reality.

Christians should learn to be Christians and understand the Golden Rule, to love other family members as themselves, to understand love, harmony, unity, helpfulness, patience and kindness.

Latter-day Saints could very well set a shining example to the world in this regard. Some members of the Church do not, but most can and many do.

If every family studied the scriptures, lived the gospel in the home, attended to their daily prayers, held family home evenings, and otherwise lived the gospel, their example would be as a beacon on a hill to all mankind.

But parents must take the initiative, both in learning how to be good parents, how to develop a righteous family circle, and how to control their own tempers and selfish tendencies; and then they must teach their children to do likewise.

It is still true that if we properly train up a child when he is small, when he is old he will hardly depart therefrom.

BEGIN AT BIRTH

The rearing of children should begin at birth. Little habits are started almost immediately afterward. This is the time to teach with love, to train in proper mental impressions, to begin even with lessons in obedience.

From youngest childhood, children should be taught the meaning of prayer. Even little ones a year old can kneel with the family in family prayer and begin to form that habit which can and probably will remain with them into adulthood.

As soon as the children learn to talk, they can be taught righteousness, truthfulness and cleanliness. They can be taught simple lessons in the gospel, but always in love and kindness.

Doesn't every child like a bedtime story? It is all well and good to tell them the classics in the fairy tales — they are a part of education — but especially should they be told bedtime stories from the scriptures and from Church history. That is essential education!

Lessons taught at that early age are not only remembered, but they are believed; hence that is the time to begin to build faith.

Families who are taught gospel principles and proper religious habits from childhood have a spirit and an attitude that are most commendable.

Children from such families expect to go on missions, marry in the temple, honor parents and live righteously. And why? Because the gospel became a part of their very souls during those early years of childhood training.

Solomon was right. Train up a child when he is young and he will keep the faith when he is old.

THE STORY HOUR

In an issue of the *Reader's Digest* a very persuasive article appeared urging parents to draw nearer to their little children by telling them bedtime stories.

James Daniel, the author, said to parents: "If you do this even a few minutes a day, the dividends will be beyond price. You will build a lasting link of shared pleasure and understanding across the generations. . . . It's really a better fortune than any amount of money you could leave your child."

What excellent advice this is! Thousands of Latter-day Saint families have done this over the years and have experienced the rich rewards that result.

But they do not limit their story telling to fairy tales, as some do. All children should know and enjoy the classic fairy tales which have become a part of our literature. But fairy tales are not enough.

Stories from the scriptures and from our Church history can equal the fascination of anything Hans Christian Andersen ever dreamed of — and more.

Parents who tell bedtime stories from the scriptures can teach the gospel to their little ones very effectively by this method, and at the same time entertain them as well.

What better opportunity is there to help little ones love Joseph Smith, Nephi, Alma, Abinadi, and Moroni, or young Samuel in the temple, or the boy Jesus and then the Christ in His adult role?

At this impressionable age our little ones may be taught the truths in story form as at few other times in their lives.

The greatest need of our people as a whole is genuine conversion to the gospel, a conversion that will bring lifelong dedication and obedience.

Why do some people go astray? Because they are not fully converted. Why is worldliness so attractive to many? Because they have not truly tasted the sweet fruits of the Tree of Life.

Jesus said we must be born again. Our hearts must be touched, our emotions stabilized, our minds instructed, so that we shall stand on solid ground in the face of temptation.

It was no idle word given by the Savior when He commanded us to search the scriptures. Is there any better way to do so than to seek out their eternal truths and retell them in story form to our impressionable little ones who ask each evening: "Tell me a story"?

Actually it is a way, not only of converting our little ones as we entertain them at bedtime, but also of converting the parents themselves as they make such a custom a part of their family routine.

PRAYING FOR THE PRESIDENT

It has been the custom of Latter-day Saints over the years to pray for the president of the Church as well as for our other leaders. This is part of sustaining the brethren.

But how do the leaders themselves feel about such prayers?

Elder Gene R. Cook, of the First Quorum of the Seventy, tells a touching story pertaining to President Kimball and his attitude toward such prayers. Wrote Elder Cook:

"It was Christmastime 1973. The traditional excitement was in the air, and particularly in Salt Lake City with the Tabernacle Choir Christmas program and other like affairs increasing that spirit.

"Our family was especially pleased as we were invited to an employee Christmas reception in the general board room of the Council of the Twelve. My wife and I and our oldest boy were invited.

"After we had shaken hands with a few of the General Authorities, we all took a glass of punch and some cookies and went over into one of the far corners to attempt to be out of the way and allow other employees the opportunity to talk to some of the brethren who were there.

"We were just beginning to feel secure in our little world of three, when all of a sudden a door in the corner where we were standing opened and in walked President Spencer W. Kimball, president of the Council of the Twelve. He, of course, greeted us, and then took our son's head in his hands to ask him if he was going on a mission. He was told that he was. President Kimball then told him that he would become a great missionary, which we considered to be a prophetic statement to be fulfilled by the faith of our son and ourselves.

"In the process, we told President Kimball of a rather humorous experience that occurred in our family during the past week. Our children had been in the habit of praying for the presiding brethren by name. Our second son was praying and said, 'Bless Pwesident Wee, Pwesident Tanno and Pwesident Womney.' He then began to go on in his prayer, having forgotten to bless lastly, President Kimball, president of the Twelve. His older brother, in a whispering tone, corrected him saying, 'You forgot President Kimball.' Whereupon, the second boy answered, 'He didn't need it tonight,' and went on and finished his prayer.

"Of course, President Kimball chuckled at the story, but then in dead seriousness pointed his finger at me and at my son and said, 'You tell your second son that he should never forget me again. We need all the prayers of the young children of the Church to sustain us. I could never do what I have to do, if it were not for their prayers.' He then told me again, 'You be sure your children pray for me every night.'

"We were tremendously pleased with those few moments with President Kimball and, even more so, for the lesson he taught us about the power of children's prayers. As he spoke the words of the Lord to us that night, little did he know that within a matter of days President Harold B. Lee would pass through the veil to the spirit world and President Kimball would be president of the Church, making those words to us even more prophetic: 'I need the prayers of every child in all the Church to sustain me.' "

SUFFER THE CHILDREN

It may be that children in Bible times were supposed to be seen and not heard, as some are today; or it may be that they were not even to be seen very much either.

Certainly they were kept back vigorously from the Savior until He rebuffed the adults and said, "Suffer little children to come unto me." It could have been quite a shock to many when He said that of such is the Kingdom of God.

Who can measure the worth of a child?

Cruelty to children is characteristic where the family concept of love and loyalty in the home has not been properly developed. It may be that in some instances the expression "the children suffer" more accurately describes the facts than "suffer the children."

It is a national disgrace in America that cruelty to children is so rapidly increasing with the breakdown in public morals. Can we ever forgive ourselves when we realize that last year there were more than a million cases of severe child abuse in this nation, with two thousand deaths among them?

But there are numerous cases of child neglect that are not classed under the category of cruelty or abuse. Neglect covers a multitude of sins, as most officials, social workers, and educators have come to know.

However, there is one field of neglect which is so widespread that every citizen might well examine his own status with respect to it: That is the field of gospel teaching, development of general spirituality, and proper character building in the home.

It is well known that true conversion to gospel principles changes people's lives; many souls are truly "born again." But how much direct gospel study and character building are provided by most parents in the home? If parents were deeply spiritual and would teach spirituality to their children, the whole face of the nation could be changed. And if character building became a regular project in every family, the rising generation could virtually bring heaven on earth.

But this is attainable only if the parents themselves are spiritual and of good character. The scripture teaches that only good trees produce good fruit and that bad trees most certainly bring forth after their kind.

It is for parents to choose. By their own examples, whether

for good or for ill, they place their children on the pathway of the future. If the wrong road is chosen, not only will the children suffer, but whole communities will suffer with them.

But if the children are properly trained and taught to love the Lord, honor righteousness and make integrity a basic standard of their lives, we then may come to understand what the Savior really had in mind as He said, "Suffer little children to come unto me, and forbid them not: for of such is the kingdom of God." (Luke 18:16.)

"AND WHEN THEY ARE OLD..."

Every grateful person should celebrate Mother's Day in its true sense, for who can adequately express full appreciation for what our mothers do for us?

Giving us life, of course, is the greatest gift of mothers, for without life, naturally there is nothing.

But what kind shall it be? Good mothers know that life is more than procreation. It includes the years that follow birth, and will depend on the kind of environment and training given during the course of that life.

To rear a child properly is quite as important as to give it life, for in the rearing lies the secret of success or failure. What was it the Savior said about certain sinners for whom it would be better if they had never been born? (3 Ne. 28:35.)

This was said about Judas: "The Son of man goeth as it is written of him: but woe unto that man by whom the Son of man is betrayed! it had been good for that man if he had not been born." (Matt. 26:24.)

The rearing of children of course is intended to be a joint effort of fathers and mothers, both of whom must unitedly establish such a desirable home atmosphere and provide such an excellent method of teaching righteousness that the little ones will grow up to become law-abiding, productive citizens, and devout followers of the Lord Jesus Christ.

For this reason the Lord has cautioned — even commanded — parents to properly teach their children so that they will love the gospel and obey it. We are to teach them to pray and walk uprightly before the Lord. Walking uprightly is one of the crying needs of humanity today, in this time of dishonesty and corruption. (D&C 68:25-28.)

President Brigham Young taught this:

"If you mothers will live your religion, then in the love and fear of God teach your children constantly and thoroughly in the way of life and salvation, training them up in the way they should go, when they are old they will not depart from it. I promise you this, it is as true as the shining sun, it is an eternal truth." (*Journal of Discourses,* 19:92.)

When the home evening was introduced by the First Presidency in 1915, President Joseph F. Smith and his counselors, Presidents Anthon H. Lund and Charles W. Penrose, made this promise:

"If the Saints obey this counsel we promise that great blessings will result. Love at home and obedience to parents will increase. Faith will be developed in the hearts of the youth of Israel, and they will gain power to combat the evil influence and temptations which beset them." (*Improvement Era,* June 1915.)

What better could father do on Mother's Day than to honor her by helping her to rear her children properly?

What better could children do than to respond in kind?

And in what manner can this be done more effectively than through regular home evenings and the companionship and spirituality required for every day of the week?

Mothers are indeed partners with God, but their work reaches its zenith only as the entire family cooperates.

PREVENTIVE THERAPY

Preventive medical care has proven to be one of the great blessings of modern civilization. Some of our worst killer diseases have been wiped out, and many thousands of lives have been saved as a result of advance precautionary treatment.

One of the outstanding examples is dreaded polio. This disease only a few years ago killed or maimed people nationwide, young and mature. Now a case is rare indeed. Polio is almost forgotten.

Another is German measles, or rubella. In one epidemic in the United States fifty thousand children died before birth or were born with serious defects. This came in 1964-1965 because their mothers fell ill with rubella. The vaccine for this disease was not licensed until 1969.

But now human carelessness enters the picture in an alarming manner. With such diseases no longer prominently before us, people have relaxed. To the horror of public health officials millions of children are no longer given the vaccines for either of these killer diseases.

A new polio epidemic could occur and take thousands of lives or leave an army of children crippled for life, our health officials say. Another rubella epidemic could occur with similar results. And why? Because of carelessness. Because preventive therapy is at present being ignored by most of the parents in the nation.

What a price some child may pay for the failure of his parents to protect him against such afflictions! Could any parents ever forgive themselves if their child was struck down, knowing that they — the parents — by a simple and easy step could have prevented it?

Now let us apply this lesson to spiritual things. Salvation in the kingdom of God is more important than anything this world has to offer. And yet there are hosts of children who are never taught the gospel in their homes. Prayer and worship are unknown to them. Often the name of Deity is heard only in profanity.

And why are the children not taught the gospel? For the same reason they are not protected against polio and rubella. Parental neglect!

There are numerous children who may go into lives of crime and corruption because they do not know a better way. Their parents are failing to fortify them against such a fate by neglecting spiritual preventive therapy, which is to teach them the gospel.

Are parents any freer of blame in one case than in another? What thoughtful parent could have any peace of mind knowing that his or her neglect had allowed a child to lead such a life?

Polio and crime! Rubella and ignorance of God! All are threats to the well being of every person. Shall we accept the available preventive therapy, or shall we drift like flotsam while spiritual and physical diseases descend upon our families?

CLEANLINESS AT HOME

Character, whether good, bad or indifferent, is usually formed in the home. And generally it develops according to the pattern laid down by the parents themselves.

There are exceptions, of course. Some of our strongest national leaders have come out of difficult home situations. Likewise, renegades occasionally come from what are considered to be the best of homes. But they are exceptions. As a rule, the home sets the pattern.

Spirituality should establish that pattern. It should prescribe the way of life for all members of the family. But only the parents can establish such an atmosphere in the home.

Moses used to teach his people that they had two choices, the good or the bad, with results that would be appropriate to the choices, also good or bad.

Joshua taught the same thing. Can anyone ever forget this great appeal to ancient Israel? "Choose you this day whom ye will serve . . . but as for me and my house, we will serve the Lord." (Josh. 24:15.)

Uncleanness in the home appears in various ways. Sometimes it is in the housekeeping itself. More than one husband has been disgusted with his family life because of poor housekeeping and left never to return again.

At times the problem is in attitudes toward truthfulness, when lying and deceit are indulged in by parents, who, by their examples, teach these same things to their children. The use of profanity is a companion evil.

Then there are the physical practices which include the use of liquor, tobacco and drugs, and even the lesser evils of tea and coffee. Statistics clearly show that most drinking and smoking youngsters have their first experience with these addictions in the home. Generally it is the drinking and smoking parents who provide the indulgence for their children. Some children begin smoking and drinking as early as four and five years of age.

And then there are the moral standards. When will all parents set the proper example of righteousness in the home? When will connubial perversions end? When will fathers cease to lay temptation in the way of their children? When will child abuse stop? What crime, short of murder, can damage the life of a child more than such abuse?

Homes are certainly the builders of the nation. They can either build or destroy individual character, too. Which mold will they cast? Which pattern will they cut?

If only all would remember Joshua and, with him and his family, choose to serve the Lord!

BAPTIZING OUR CHILDREN

The Lord holds parents accountable for the education of their children in gospel principles. What He says in section 68 of the Doctrine and Covenants should surely convert any sincere person.

Part of that responsibility is found in preparing our little ones for the time when they may be baptized at the age of eight years. They need to know why they are baptized. They must have faith to accompany that ordinance. That comes by teaching.

And who is to teach them?

It is a family responsibility which rests heavily upon the parents of those children.

From infancy our little ones should be trained in the gospel. As soon as they can understand the language they should be taught its simple truths. Bedtime stories form one of our best means of doing so for the little ones.

Parents may well choose appropriate stories from the scriptures, from Church history, from journals of their own forefathers, or even from the personal experiences of the parents themselves. Told with the proper objective, with testimony being borne to them by their parents, such stories will convert our little ones, and thus develop faith.

As children grow older they will be taught about baptism. They may witness the baptism of their older brothers and sisters, and be encouraged to look forward to the day when this blessing will come to them.

But the seeds of faith must be planted well in advance, and the soil must be prepared even before the seed is sown.

Parents who fail in this responsibility do their children a great disservice.

YOUTH-PARENT PROBLEMS

For many years students of youthful misbehavior have said that our problem is more with the parents than with the youth themselves. As it is now, some parents have literally given up in the face of the extreme misconduct of their children.

Reports from police and school officials are discouraging as far as many of America's young people are concerned. It is indeed distressing to learn that "tens of thousands of runaways, pregnant girls, and disobedient children are being warehoused in jails, detention centers and foster homes," as *U.S. News and World Report* announced.

It is heartbreaking to know that television sets exhibiting constant violence have a greater impact upon young people than many parents are able to exert.

The increased use of drugs and alcohol among the youngsters, the lowering age of immorality, the mounting vandalism, the atrocious attacks by vicious students upon their schoolteachers, all are marks of a rapidly deteriorating situation. A U.S. study reveals that suicides now begin to involve children eleven years of age and younger. The entire picture seems utterly incredible. But it is true.

The situation cannot be allowed to continue. After all, the adults run this country. We must admit that many have set bad examples for their children in many respects, lifted all restraints, and have become more interested in their own pursuits than in the welfare of their offspring.

But the forces for good — those which build character, integrity, obedience to law, and mutual respect — can correct the situation. However, to suggest — as some are doing — that since the birth rate is steadily declining, we might just wait a few years until there will be fewer children and hence fewer problems, makes no sense and is defeatist.

The first and most potent force for good is the family. If the family will only take the trouble to be a family, if parents will take their proper place in love, kindness, and firmness, they can establish a home discipline that will work. Some parents of adolescents may laugh at that and say it is too late, and it may be too late in many instances, for proper family life really begins with the infancy of the children.

If parents will only reintroduce genuine character into the home, if they will regard the rearing of their children as their first and major responsibility, and bring in the gospel of Christ to help them, they can overcome the problem. They can so strengthen and train their little ones that the children will resist the peer pressures that otherwise could take them into sin.

The schools must reorient themselves and look at discipline differently. Also a close coalition between teachers and parents can work wonders. We have the PTA all across the country. It has done great things. Why not make it work now in this emergency? Why should not every parent become actively associated with it, and give to teachers the kind of support they need? PTA properly directed can go far in solving this problem.

And then there is the Church. The scripture asks, "Is any thing too hard for the Lord?" (Gen. 18:14.) Let the power of conversion to the gospel of Christ take over in every home, and hearts will be changed and evil ways will be corrected. That is, if we have the faith and courage to apply it!

Home, school, church. There is no power stronger than the power for good these three can provide.

RELIGION AND DRUGS

Children should be taught to love and respect God as a means of fighting the drug and alcohol menace.

So said one of the nation's principal experts on drug and liquor abuse.

Ashton Brisolara, executive director of the Committee on Alcoholism and Drug Abuse for New Orleans, La., spoke at the annual University of Utah clinic on drug dependencies.

He is of the opinion that "many alcoholics and drug abusers are home made" and are the result of a lack of discipline in the family.

The health educator said he is greatly concerned over the rising incidence of alcoholism and alcohol abuse, but expressed hope that it can be curbed. He said the most effective way is through education and strong family relations.

"I feel that parents give their children too much of everything — too much money and luxuries. They give them the world on a silver platter," he said.

The visitor said alcohol and other drug abuse is frequently symptomatic of many family problems. Good family communication, parental example, not showing preferences between family members, helping children to learn how to work, and the use of discipline are some of the answers. Children also should be taught to love and respect God, he said.

"You don't guide them by saying yes all the time. They must have good example. If parents drink or get drunk, how can they expect anything different from their children? If they are always taking pills unnecessarily, how can they expect anything different from their children?" he asked.

It is a fact. The gospel of Christ can save all people, not only from major sins but from such habits as drug and liquor abuse. Children taught properly by their parents never need fall to the seductions of these evils.

And as usual, the home — if it is a good home — is the answer. Let us strengthen our family circles.

THE BETTER WAY

Industry will tell us that "on the job training" is the most effective way to equip employees for the business they hope to follow. If "on the job training" is best for industry, is it not best also for the home?

The responsibility of parents is to provide that particular kind of teaching and instruction for their children. Dare they hope to escape this obligation?

In the world of nature, "on the job training" is seen everywhere. The mother bird teaches young ones to fly. The lioness teaches her cubs to hunt for food. Nearly all mothers in nature are willing to fight and die to protect their little ones.

But as the Savior said while speaking of the fowls of the air and the lilies of the field, "Are ye not much better than they?"

Absentee parents are like absentee teachers at school, or absentee supervisors in a factory, or junketing lawmakers. When they are not home, they are not "on the job," and can lose some of their effectiveness.

Money magazine in January 1980 reported that 28 percent of working couples have little children in the home. Where is the "on the job" training there? In 49 percent of American homes there are working wives. This includes fourteen U.S. congressmen's wives each of whom had more than one million dollars in real estate sales last year.

Parents themselves must learn to be of good character. They must repent from permissiveness, irreligious tendencies, drinking, smoking, pornography, drugs and other character-destroying factors.

Only by their own good examples and by daily "on the job training" can they truly build righteousness into the souls of their children.

NOTHING LIKE A HOME

Attitudes toward crime and criminals change almost with each generation. For a time incarceration was considered the only real answer to crime. Then came the rehabilitation concept, where efforts were made to teach criminals how to live properly out of prison.

Studies indicate that for habitual criminals, after all is said, prison is the best answer because in so many cases the rehabilitation does not work, and even "reformed" criminals become frequent repeaters, discarding all the training they have received while confined. They would rather steal than work.

The Rand Corporation of Santa Monica, Calif., recently made a study of methods of dealing with felons. They discovered many interesting things, among which was, of course, that the repeat offender is the most difficult to handle.

The study showed that one group of only forty-nine offenders perpetrated a total of 10,500 crimes, or an average of 214 per offender. The criminal career of each offender averaged about twenty years, half of which time was spent in prison. Each offender committed an average of twenty major felonies per year when he was free. The crimes ranged from burglary and drug sales to aggravated assault and rape.

One of the frightening things about the report was that only 12 percent of the reported crimes ended in arrests.

The debate will no doubt continue over whether criminals should simply be kept off the streets by longer and more severe sentences, or whether rehabilitation really works. Such rehabilitation has its points, but it is nevertheless agreed that a great many criminals who take the treatment are not cured.

The Rand study showed that people who are gainfully employed are less liable to commit crimes. Other studies certainly show that young people who receive proper home training have far less tendency to violence and crime.

As the experts have studied the entire criminal spectrum, they have universally come to one vital and important conclusion: there is no substitute for a good home, where parents are interested in their children, where the parents themselves are righteous, law-abiding citizens, and where the gospel is taught to young people — and lived.

It is the same lesson which mankind has refused to learn over the ages. It has been repeated for centuries. God and home are the most important influences for good in anyone's life. Why do so many refuse to admit it and accept it?

ATTEND TITHING SETTLEMENT

At the close of each year we are invited to attend tithing settlement at the bishop's office. It is expected of every Latter-day Saint, whether a tithe payer or not.

As we approach the end of the year it would be well for each member of the Church, young and old alike, to examine his tithing record to determine if a full and honest settlement has been made.

It is well that every Latter-day Saint remember that tithing is a law of God, and was made so in the earliest times. The ancient scriptures reveal this.

Can we forget the explanation of this law which was made by Malachi? He declares the commandment: "Bring ye all the tithes into the storehouse." And then he explains the blessings that will come as a result.

As Malachi presents this law, he says that its purpose is "that there may be meat in mine house." (Mal. 3:10.)

Various presidents of the Church have explained that tithing is the Lord's law of revenue by which the work of the kingdom may be financed and made effective.

It is more than "meat," however, although that is an important part of it. Tithing has played a vital role in the Welfare Program of the Church, and this program, in turn, is becoming more and more important as the difficult times of these latter days increase.

But for us, the kingdom requires more than that there may be "meat in mine house." We also must build the house to put it in. And we must operate it. We need more than storehouses, and with our worldwide expansion, we also require more missions, more chapels, more temples, more school facilities and more of nearly everything. This is all covered in that expression "meat in mine house."

The promise of Malachi is impressive also. Not only does he say that the windows of heaven will be opened upon us in a most generous manner, but "I will rebuke the devourer for your sakes," that he will not destroy us or our livelihood. (Mal. 3:11.)

There can be a deep meaning in the rebuke to the devourer, for the devil, who is the arch-devourer, would seek to consume our homes if possible, destroy our loved ones and break up our family circles. Do we not need a rebuke of evil in this regard?

Little children should be taught to pay tithing from their earliest years. They should be allowed to earn some little amount, if by nothing more than keeping a room neat or picking up the toys, so that they will have a basis for paying tithing.

Teaching them to pay without providing them with the opportunity to pay almost becomes an aimless exercise.

Every member of the family should be a tithe payer. A lesson on tithing would be most worthwhile as tithing settlement day comes near the end of December. It could well form the theme of an entire family home evening, with practical teaching in the principle being provided by the parents.

Tithing is a law of God. Let us all observe it.

SCREENS FOR OUR HOMES

Most families use screens of one kind or another. Some are set up for home movies, some are necessary for privacy, but most are found on our TV sets.

Every family needs still another kind of screen, one that will filter out the evils that come into the home, so often unawares. In other words, each family needs a censorship system of its own.

We need to be a part of our communities of course, and do all we can to improve them. But what shall we do when the community brings evils into our most sacred precincts, our living rooms, where we teach our little ones righteousness?

The most persistent invaders come through radio and television. The need to censor them before they reach our youngsters becomes more demanding daily. But it is difficult to do.

TV now mixes previews of future attractions between segments of scheduled programs. No matter how good the main shows may be, no one can tell when, at any moment, a repulsive preview of some seductive or violent film will be thrust before our eyes as an advertisement.

No one can say that these advertisements do not have an effect. Otherwise they would not be shown.

The seduction and the violence are not taken out of them, hence these previews are as damaging to the youth as the feature itself would be, except, thank heaven, that they are abbreviated.

Some of these previews are frightening in their evil effect and in and of themselves are degrading. How can parents censor such as that when they come on so unexpectedly?

In movies G or PG ratings were helpful at one time, but they are no longer dependable. They have been watered down and weakened. Many films so labeled are completely unfit for family consumption. So the ratings do parents little, if any, good.

With TV it is even worse, for there we have no ratings at all. Must a parent sit through each TV program with a child and turn off the set when things get rough, even in the middle of a program?

Or must parents discard the TV set altogether? This may not be the answer either, for many good things do come on the screen.

Since broadcasters give so little selective help on behalf of young people, parents must devise their own system of censorship. Above all they must protect their children. Exposing them to evil will not fortify them against it, as some say. That is folly, for evil exposure actually is temptation.

Parents should no more allow bad programs to warp the minds of their children than they would invite a teacher of sin to come into the home and there personally defile the family circle.

LAW AND OBEDIENCE

FIRST THINGS FIRST

The message of today's general conference sessions is clear and to the point: "Keep the commandments."

The clarion call comes as the General Authorities speak: "Keep the commandments."

Although each speaker presents his subject in his own individual manner, the substance of each address is always: "Keep the commandments." And why? Because there is no other way to true happiness, no other way to salvation.

Our obedience must be consistent. There is no room for vacillating in dealing with the Lord. He condemns lukewarm attitudes and compromising efforts to serve both God and mammon at the same time.

In these days of establishing goals and priorities, the Saints are forcefully reminded that only one thing can be first in our lives if we hope to please the Lord, and that is devotion to Him.

When the Lord gave the commandment to seek Him first, He spoke of our daily affairs, our worries over food, raiment and shelter, the things about which we concern ourselves most.

But He gave a marvelous promise as He did so: "Your Heavenly Father knoweth that ye have need of all these things. But seek ye first the kingdom of God, and his righteousness; *and all these things shall be added unto you.*" (Matt. 6:32-33.)

That promise has been renewed consistently by our modern prophet-leaders. For example, President Joseph F. Smith said: "The promise is that if we will obey the laws of God, if we put our trust in Him, if we will draw near to Him, He will draw near to us and He will reward us with His favor and blessing."

President Heber J. Grant promised peace, prosperity and financial success to the sincere tithe payer.

President George Albert Smith promised joy and peace "if we stay on the Lord's side of the line."

President David O. McKay taught: "Conformity with the Lord's word will invariably contribute to man's happiness and salvation."

President Joseph Fielding Smith said: "If members of the Church will obey the divine commandments they will be in perfect accord with the Spirit of the Lord and they will not be deceived."

President Harold B. Lee taught: "As one studies the commandments of God it seems crystal clear that the all-important thing is not where we live but whether or not our hearts are pure."

And President Spencer W. Kimball has many times over the past decades asked the Saints to "keep the commandments."

One of the sad things about humanity is that few are willing to learn from the past. Through the centuries, both time and events have proven what the prophets have said: Only by obedience to the commandments may mankind achieve a proper well-being.

God's great desire is to bless us that we may become like Him, but He cannot do so unless we obey the laws upon which His blessings are predicated.

OUR SABBATH OBSERVANCE

President McKay was a great advocate of Sabbath Day observance, as are our other leaders.

He also was a strong advocate of attendance at our meetings on the Sabbath Day. At one time he said that he could not understand how anyone could keep the Sabbath Day holy without attending our Sunday meetings.

He further said:

"Is it better to cherish church ideals on Sunday or to indulge in Sunday sports?

"One great purpose in observing the Sabbath Day is 'that thou mayest more fully keep thyself unspotted from the world.' "

And then he said: "Keeping the Sabbath Day holy is a law of God. You cannot transgress the law of God without circumscribing your spirit."

Added to that he taught that since the first day of the week commemorates the greatest event in all history — Christ's resurrection — we cannot ignore or violate the spirit of that day with impunity.

Attendance at our Sunday meetings is all-important to spiritual growth. It is in the house of the Lord that the Holy Spirit abides. We can feel it the instant we enter the doorway.

It is in the services of the Church that we sing the songs of Zion, hymns to the Lord our God. And the songs of the righteous are as prayers unto Him.

It is there that we pray with our brothers and sisters. It is there that we teach and are taught the principles of the gospel. It is there that we renew our covenants which help us always to remember Him.

It is in these meetings that we humbly partake of the sacrament of the Lord's Supper, which itself is a commandment of God.

Sacrament meetings were instituted by the direction of the Lord. The Saints were commanded to attend them regularly, there to offer their oblations to the Most High and to "confess their sins before their brethren."

The spirit and purpose of the sacrament meeting is such that no one should miss it. Visiting friends and relatives, pleasure-seeking or other self-centered pursuits will never be accepted by the Lord as substitutes for these meetings.

The Lord has made it clear that no one can be saved in ignorance. Therefore He also has provided a Sunday School organization in which the gospel is to be taught to young and old alike every Sabbath Day.

All members of the Church therefore should attend Sunday School. It is the duty of priesthood-holders particularly to actively support it, to encourage their families to attend, and to be there themselves.

Priesthood meetings, held also on the Sabbath, are likewise mighty in their spiritual influence. Those holding the priesthood, of course, should regularly attend them. Those ordained are under covenant to live by every word that proceedeth from the mouth of God.

The Almighty commands observance of the Sabbath. He likewise commands attendance at our meetings. Should not every priesthood holder respond?

The Lord teaches that if we accept His commandments with a doubtful heart and keep them with slothfulness we shall be damned (D&C 58). Does that merely refer to "the other fellow"?

The Sabbath is a day of rest, but it is also a day of worship. And who can be saved in the Lord's kingdom without worship?

Can we worship Him while playing on the golf course, or while fishing a stream or hiking in the mountains or frolicking on the beach? Can we worship Him by sitting at home reading the Sunday newspaper or watching TV?

Latter-day Saints must waken to the realities of their religion and recognize that God means business when He commands us to obey Him. Salvation can be lost by default.

WE ARE COMMANDED

Giving offense to God is a most serious thing, and He tells us that we do offend Him by our disobedience. In fact He says that the only ones who do not offend Him are "those who confess . . . his hand in all things, and obey his commandments" (D&C 59:21).

One of those commandments is that we honor the Sabbath Day, and keep it holy.

Still another is that we shall go to our meetings on that day and there offer our oblations and our sacraments unto the Most High (D&C 59:12).

There is still another yet with regard to the Lord's Day: "On this day thou shalt do none other thing, only let thy food be prepared with singleness of heart that thy fasting may be perfect, or, in other words, that thy joy may be full." (D&C 59:13.)

In the covenant of the priesthood we read that we must live by every word that proceedeth forth from the mouth of God. (D&C 84.)

In the Sermon on the Mount we are told that not everyone that calls to Him, Lord, Lord, as though to profess some degree of allegiance, shall enter into the kingdom of Heaven, but only those who do the will of the Father.

And the will of the Father includes observance of a sacred Sabbath.

What blessings may be expected by those who offend God deliberately?

How many who believe they are true Christians do offend Him? Is it possible for us to be true Christians and yet flout the Savior's law of the Sabbath?

All of the presidents of the Church have urged strongly that the Latter-day Saints honor the Sabbath.

In the days of President McKay the First Presidency issued a special message on the Sabbath which was printed in a pamphlet and widely distributed. Among other things this message said:

"The Sabbath is not just another day on which we merely rest from work, free to spend it as our lightmindedness may suggest. It is an holy day, the Lord's Day, to be spent as a day of worship and reverence. All matters extraneous thereto should be shunned. . . .

"Latter-day Saints with a testimony of the Gospel and a knowledge of the spiritual blessings that come from keeping the Sabbath, will never permit themselves to make it a shopping day, an activity that has no place in a proper observance of the Holy Day of the Lord."

They spoke vigorously against all Sabbath-breaking activities, and called attention to the fact that this law was given that the Saints might "more fully keep themselves unspotted from the world."

What sincere believer in God would offend Him? What thoughtful person would assume the awesome responsibility of setting aside His Sabbath Day?

GETTING A FRESH START

Although many people do not make New Year's resolutions, and although many both make and break them, the New Year does give us an opportunity for a fresh start.

Everyone needs a fresh start from time to time. Special occasions provide for such new beginnings, and New Year's is one of them.

Is anybody so satisfied with himself that he cannot improve? Isn't improvement the very essence of progress? And don't we all need to progress in life, in building good character, in caring for our families, in sustaining the work of the Lord?

New Year's also gives us a good reason to review the covenants we have made with God. Each member of the Church has made them.

In solemn moments, in sacred places, we have entered agreements with the Lord pertaining to our relationship to Him.

He offers us a more abundant life in this world than we would otherwise have. He offers us eternal life in the world to come. He offers us happy family circles, not just in mortality but in the hereafter. He promises us such growth, development and improvement that eventually we can become like Him. To what extent? "Unto the measure of the stature of the fulness of Christ." (Eph. 4:13.)

But to achieve that, we must fit into His pattern, obey His laws, and practice each of His divine principles. To help us be true to this objective, He placed us under covenants.

In baptism, we agree that we will serve Him to the end. In the sacrament of the Lord's supper, we agree that we will always remember Him and keep His commandments. These covenants are especially sacred, not only because they are made between us and our Heavenly Father, but because they are based upon Christ's atonement.

The Atonement was the most important thing that has ever happened. We should remember that in it, Jesus suffered such pain that He bled from every pore.

As we eat the broken bread, representing His torn flesh, and as we drink of the cup, reminding us of His blood shed on the cross, we seal our covenants with God.

Our partaking of the sacrament is the very act by which we do seal those covenants. By His torn flesh, by His blood shed in agony, do we solemnize our pledge to obey.

We also agree in the oath and covenant of the priesthood to live by every word that proceeds from the mouth of God. This includes chastity, honesty, devotion, integrity, honoring the Sabbath, paying our tithes and offerings, caring for the sick and distressed, aiding the poor and unfortunate, and all other phases of the gospel.

At this New Year's would it not be well for us to review our own performance in the light of these covenants? Do our lives measure up to our promises? Does our obedience meet the Lord's expectation?

Why not use New Year's Day as the time to make one great and permanent resolution: to study the covenants we have made and then honor them?

"Fear God, and keep his commandments: for this is the whole duty of man." (Eccl. 12:13.)

DO-IT-YOURSELF RELIGION

Are people free to set up religious movements in whatever way they please? Do such movements save souls? Are they acceptable to God?

At the moment there are many such movements getting under way. According to the *U.S. News & World Report,* they are "spreading rapidly, attracting millions of believers to the emotional yet simple devotions that many regard as a rejection of older forms of worship."

The magazine then goes on to say:

"Catholics are attending faith healings and ecstatic prayer groups reminiscent of backwoods revivals. Young Protestants and Jews are making up their own services. . . . "

There is a crying need for good religion in America. Gallup polls claim that 95 percent of all Americans believe in a God of some kind. And yet only 44 percent have enough confidence in "organized religion" to belong to it. Nearly as many deliberately avoid any church.

It is encouraging indeed that so many, especially among the youth of the land, seek religious expression. But how sad it is that they are misled or at least mistaken in their concepts of what is acceptable to God.

It is one thing to set up a system of worship and follow it. It is quite another to have acceptance on the part of the Almighty.

The Lord is the author of free agency, and certainly allows everyone to worship when, how and what he likes. But the question is, in which religion is there true salvation? Will just any church lead to heaven? The answer is No!

Youth who make up their own religions, like those in established churches, expect to live after death and possibly face their Maker. Gallup says that 71 percent of all Americans believe in a hereafter.

But the Lord laid down some rigid specifics about His gospel, all of which must be observed to earn the reward. Salvation is not a matter of belief alone, nor of a confession of a faith.

Most people have a misconception of what is meant in the expression "by grace are ye saved." They also mistake the meaning of the scripture which says that faith without works is dead.

The grace in salvation is that Christ, out of sheer mercy and love for mankind, died willingly that we might live. His gospel plan is given us freely through His grace. But the gospel plan, once received, must be lived and worked and used as a pattern of daily activity.

In Christ's day not every church would do. Not the Pharisees, not the Sadducees, not the Essenes, not the Hellenists, not the Zealots. There was no salvation in any of them. When the Lord denounced their doctrine He said that their worship was in vain — without value. (Matt.15.)

Today's youth — and everyone else for that matter — must realize that Christ has but one Church, headed by apostles and prophets; that He has but one gospel; that there must be baptism, but only one form of baptism, and that there must be obedience to all the behavior guides which appear in the Sermon on the Mount and elsewhere in His scripture.

There is salvation in no other way. Freedom of religion may be great, but if it is the wrong religion, it will not save.

KNOWING ONE'S DUTY

One of the many impressive revelations given by the Lord to the Prophet Joseph Smith is that which we call section 107 of the Doctrine and Covenants. It is a great revelation and ends on a significant note:

"Wherefore, now let every man learn his duty, and to act in

the office in which he is appointed, in all diligence. He that is slothful shall not be counted worthy to stand, and he that learns not his duty and shows himself not approved shall not be counted worthy to stand" (D&C 107:99-100).

In commenting on this passage at one time, President David O. McKay said:

"Two principles are inherent in individual responsibility; first, the learning, knowing what one's duty is; second, to act in all diligence in the performance of that duty. The man who knows what his duty is and fails to perform it is not true to himself; he is not true to his fellowmen."

President Harry S Truman once said this:

"I studied the lives of great men and famous women, and I found that the men and women who got to the top were those who did the jobs they had in hand with everything they had of energy and enthusiasm and hard work."

With our assignments in the Church especially we should devote our best attention to the work in hand. The Lord should not be second best in anyone's mind, and neither should His work.

He tells us that the glory of God is intelligence, and certainly, therefore, He wants us to be intelligent in the way we do our work. Hence He tells us to learn our duty well, and work in it diligently.

HE EXPECTS DEVOTION

The Lord is consistent in His gospel requirements. He is also very realistic, for He realizes that we can become like Him only through obedience to the plan of salvation.

Lukewarm performance will not save anyone. Being slothful can only bring condemnation (D&C 58:26-29). Mere membership in the Church alone will do us little good, for faith without works is dead. And especially is faith dead if it is not only without works but also if it lacks a believing heart. Mere professions mean little.

It is no play on words when the Lord tells us to serve Him with all our "heart, might, mind and strength" (D&C 4:2). Neither are they idle words when the Lord asks us to love Him with our whole heart and soul.

He expects us to comply with these commandments. And why is He so strict?

Simply because we cannot attain perfection by imperfect means. He commands that we become like Him. To do so must be our aim. It is our destiny. That is the purpose of our very existence. Many people wonder where we came from, why we are alive, and whether there is life after death.

The whole purpose of our existence is to become like God, just as He commanded (Matt. 5:48). The gospel is the plan; Jesus Christ is our pattern. Unless we follow Him and His direction we do not reach the objective.

The gospel is one of works — hard work at times — and never-ending devotion. Faith must be combined with our works, for as Paul said, we must work out our salvation. It is an endless task.

AGED SISTER BROWN

Mary Brown was a widow, seventy-four years old. Having reared her family of six, she now resided alone in a little cottage on Adams Street. Her only income was her Social Security check. Her friends were few but her arthritis pains were many. She was not happy.

Her family neglected her and seldom came near. No one

else did, either, except for the Relief Society teachers, and even they came only once a month.

Inflation shrank her income almost daily. Not being skilled in handling her money, it sometimes was gone before the end of the month. Her diet was poor, and that was reflected in her failing health.

She had some illnesses, and occasionally over-medicated herself because she misunderstood her doctor's instructions. Her family had urged her to go to a rest home, but she liked her independence and wanted to stay in her own little house as long as she was able to care for herself.

She had no entertainment, or hobbies, or other interests to occupy her mind. She had no TV as other people had, nor even an AM radio. She never read a newspaper either. She couldn't afford a subscription. Her life was empty. On Sundays, in good weather, she would make the effort to walk to church, but could not attend in inclement seasons since she had no means of transportation. Loneliness was her greatest enemy.

Then there was Sister Jones, a happy lady with a life filled with interests and as many activities as her seventy-two years would permit. She had learned to enjoy good books and she read by the hour. She visited her neighbors too and told some of them about the gospel. Within a two-year period through these visits she had brought three families into the Church. She would teach them all she could and then would call in the stake missionaries to complete the instruction. What a joy this labor was to her! What good things may be accomplished even through the friendly visits of a cheerful elderly lady!

She had no more income than did Sister Brown but the Relief Society of her ward had taught her how to budget, and showed her many little household hints which made living easier than it otherwise would have been.

Sister Jones went to the temple twice a week. She was able to attend her Sunday meetings through the kindness of a thoughtful neighbor who furnished her transportation. Hers was a good life. She found that aging could be pleasant and profitable.

What made these two lives so different?

First of all, kindly neighbors showed Sister Jones that life had much to offer, even at her age. They taught her that service to others brings much happiness, so she responded and found out for herself that in service to other people, especially those less fortunate than herself, there is much joy and satisfaction. Life was no burden to her. She constantly created opportunities to show kindness to other people. She never felt sorry for herself, for she was too busy.

Sister Jones also had a thoughtful bishop who provided bimonthly entertainments in the ward cultural hall for all people in the ward over sixty-five years of age. For the housebound, the Relief Society provided daily visits, although brief, by neighboring women. They came to Sister Jones's home, too, brightening her days as well.

She learned that the busier she kept herself, the healthier she was both mentally and physically. No senility was detected in her as it had begun to appear in lonely, inactive Sister Brown.

Could Sister Brown be made as happy as Sister Jones? She could be, by all means, but it would require a good deal of cooperation on the part of her family, her Relief Society and herself.

She would have to acquire interests outside of her home. She would have to make the decision to fit into a new pattern of living and actually look for and find people whom she could help, if in nothing more than a friendly, cheerful visit. There are plenty of other lonely people besides herself. They would welcome her. No longer need she sit at home worrying about herself.

But a cooperative effort would have to create this new life for Sister Brown. Would the family do its part? Would the people in the Church? Would her ward do as well as Sister Jones's ward had done? They were good people, but their interests were elsewhere, not in Sister Brown.

Like her they too would need re-orientation. They too would need to learn to love their neighbors as themselves — and serve and cheer them — even the poor and the lonely — even Sister Brown.

THE BEST OF BOTH

We often speak of having the best of two worlds. That is what every person may have who is willing to serve the Lord and keep His commandments.

The Savior said that if we serve Him we shall not only live, but we shall live more abundantly. That applies both to this mortal world and the world to come.

To serve Him here gives us an abundance of the good things of life and spares us from the afflictions which accompany the sinful life. When we think of the evils and diseases that come from violations of the Word of Wisdom, when we think of the distress that invades families where "love at home" is lacking, we realize truly that living the gospel does bring peace and joy in our present estate.

But think, too, of the abundant life in the eternal world for those who keep "their second estate." There the Lord promises us "all that he has," glories and advancement forever, the extension of family life, again forever, and the possibility of even becoming perfect as our Father in Heaven is perfect. (Matt. 5:48.)

We can have the best of both worlds if only we will be sincere in our religion and truly serve the Lord.

FATHER AND MOTHER

WHAT IS A FATHER?

We can hardly think of father without also thinking of fatherhood, and all that it means.

Fatherhood means family; it means children, and rearing them the right way; it means instructing them about our Heavenly Father, and what His fatherhood means.

When the Lord made mankind, He laid down a plan whereby the race would be perpetuated. He was particularly interested in this process; that is why He made the earth; that is why He placed us here.

He was perpetuating His own species and that for eternity. We are indeed the children of God. We are truly destined to become like Him. Only our own disobedience can stand in the way.

His work is to bring to pass the immortality and eternal life of man, and that means to become like Him. In fact, we are given one of His commandments which fully proves that this is possible, but not only possible — expected! "Be ye therefore perfect, even as your Father which is in heaven is perfect." That is the law.

In seeking to bring about our eternal life, the Lord has given us every opportunity and facility for achieving it. He has left nothing undone. Not only has He given us life and health and strength, a glorious planet on which to live, intelligence, and faith in Him, but He has given us a pattern of life. It is the gospel which is the "formula" by which we can reach our ultimate destiny.

We have a great lesson in the fatherhood of God, for in it He provides for us, outlines the way of life, and helps us in every way to achieve it. That lesson becomes the pattern whereby we begin our eternal development right here on earth.

Here we must learn of Him. Here we must obey Him. Here we must exert every effort to emulate His example. As His children, we are His family, and He cares for us as such.

We who are fathers also must fit into the family program. There should be no fathers without matrimony and family life. Otherwise we violate the law of God.

Our example then, as seen in our Heavenly Father, is to provide a wholesome home life for our loved ones here on earth. We will care for our families, support them, teach them by example and by precept, and honor all the virtues.

If there is anything virtuous, lovely or of good report or praiseworthy, we must seek after those things.

We hope for peace on earth these days, when it appears that Satan is having another violent fling. But we can have peace, every one of us, in our own homes, within our own family circles, if we will.

If each father will take the lead and provide good family conditions, if he himself will be honorable, humble, productive of all that is good, if he will set a pattern of love at home and worship God in that home, we shall have a peace which is totally unattainable in any other way. That is what fatherhood means!

HOME AND PRIESTHOOD

The family is the basic unit of society, but it is also the basic unit of the Church. And more than that, it is fundamental to our eternal exaltation as well.

Did not Paul say that the man is not without the woman, neither the woman without the man in the Lord? And was he not speaking of the marriage relationship, the foundation of the family? (1 Cor. 11:11.)

Seeing the family unit in its true perspective is vital to our proper understanding of the gospel of Christ. We must realize that in truth we are saved on a family basis. We can become fully "like your Father which is in heaven" only in that way.

No man, no woman, is exalted in the presence of God as a single individual, that is, unmarried. Temple marriage has an eternal significance far beyond the view of most people. It is not a fad among Latter-day Saints. It is the foundation of the eternal family unit which becomes the heart and core of our eventual exaltation with God. It will be offered to every faithful person.

But that eternal family unit has its source in the priesthood for its sealing power binds the family together.

Men are given the priesthood to *use*, but only in righteousness. And where? In the Church? By all means! In the family also? Most definitely yes! (D&C 121:34-40.)

But is there one phase of priesthood to be exercised in the Church and another in the family? Certainly not! The family, being the basic unit of the Church, must enjoy the same influence of the priesthood as does the Church.

If we can properly view the family as the basic unit of the Church, and realize that the priesthood should be exercised with equal righteousness in both, we begin to see the entire purpose of our lives in the proper light.

The Lord has given presidency in his work to the priesthood. That presidency pertains to both family and Church. The priesthood is given to the husband and father. He presides — in righteousness — in the home. At the same time he may be the presiding officer in his ward or stake — possibly a bishop or a stake president.

He may be a quorum president, or the head of some auxiliary group. But he serves by virtue of the same priesthood, obtained by the same laying on of hands by those who have the right to ordain.

When presiding by virtue of the priesthood, righteousness must always prevail. That righteousness will be characterized by kindness, patience, long suffering and temperance, but also by faith, virtue, knowledge, charity, humility, diligence and god-liness! (D&C 4:5-6.)

As we would foster these principles in our Church positions, so we must see that they establish the atmosphere of our homes.

Then, as the priesthood holder, the father will be kind to his wife and children. He will be fair and just and Christlike in his relationships with them all.

He will be a man of virtue, and hold to personal purity as he would to life itself. President David O. McKay said: "Chastity is the crown of beautiful womanhood, and self-control is the source of true manhood, not indulgence. Undue sexual indulgence whets the passion and creates morbid desire. . . . The marriage covenant does not give the man the right to enslave her (his wife) or to abuse her or to use her merely for the gratification of his passion. Your marriage ceremony does not give you that right." (*Gospel Ideals* [Salt Lake City: The Improvement Era, 1953], page 471.)

The president taught, as do the scriptures, that a man must "cleave unto his wife" and to "none else," and added, "Christ's ideal pertaining to marriage is the unbroken home. Conditions that cause divorce are violations of his divine teachings." (*Gospel Ideals,* page 470; D&C 42:22.)

The priesthood bearer in the home will foster knowledge, as the scripture says; that is, he will encourage study of the gospel on the part of members of the family. Also, we are told to study all good books. (D&C 109:7.) What better thing can we do in our family circles than to seek an understanding of sound principles and then learn to obey them?

He will promote temperance — excluding extremes of thought and action. He will have charity for all, inside and outside the home.

He will be diligent — that is, an earnest worker, a good provider for his family, and a faithful advocate of clean and wholesome living and observance of all gospel principles. (D&C 84:44.)

He will live a Christlike life as he achieves the godliness required by the scripture. If every home was headed by a Christlike husband and father, we would soon eliminate family quarrels, selfishness, divorce, and juvenile delinquency within the home, and crime and sin of every description outside of the home.

With the influence of such a man in every family circle we soon would rear a generation like the City of Enoch. Righteousness would prevail everywhere.

And is not that what God wants? Does he not command us all to become perfect as he is? (Matt. 5:48.)

Then should not the priesthood holder in the home seek to establish just such a situation under his own roof, and then exert his Christlike influence in the community as well?

"As the priesthood goes, so goes the family" is a maxim of truth. If the priesthood holder lives a Christlike life, as Solomon said, the family will hardly depart from it.

And then as this sacred unit is projected into eternity, we shall reap all the blessings the Lord has in store for the faithful, for that indeed is the ultimate promise. (D&C 84:35-39.)

FATHER'S OPPORTUNITY

God has given to parents on earth three great responsibilities: to reproduce ourselves under proper marriage vows; to rear our children in the way of truth; and to be kind to each other in the bonds of Christian family life.

Fathers are given the initiative in home building. They must seek a wife. They must provide the proper home environment, and they must preside in the family circle.

Mothers are indeed the helpmeets of their husbands. When husbands abdicate their rightful and righteous role, then usually mothers of necessity take over to prevent a chaotic situation in the home.

But fathers are given the presidency of the home in righteousness. Mothers and children cooperate also in righteousness and give fealty to him as he gives fealty to his Heavenly Father.

Under circumstances such as this, the ideal home may evolve. Proper objectives and goals are established. Children are correctly taught, and mothers are honored and respected — and dearly loved — by all concerned.

In these homes the gospel is taught and literally becomes a way of life. It is understood by all that we are the children of our Heavenly Father and that we are commanded to so order our lives that we shall eventually become perfect even as He is. (Matt. 5:48.)

To have such a home is impossible unless the father does his part. Likewise it is impossible unless mother also fills her role.

Then cooperation is the watchword — cooperation in a partnership of parenthood, but also in a partnership with God.

A good marriage is basic in the first place. Both parties in the marriage must work toward its success. This can be accomplished only in an atmosphere of complete trust, integrity, and sincere love. This is what God expects of us.

Our objective of becoming Christlike must ever be in our minds, and that cannot be achieved unless as separate individuals we seek to become like Him.

We must love our neighbors as ourselves — and our family members are our closest neighbors.

We must do unto others — including and especially our family members — as we would be done by. No family can be truly successful without obeying these two basic commandments.

And then as the Lord says we must "remember faith, virtue, knowledge, temperance, patience, brotherly kindness, godliness, charity, humility, diligence." (D&C 4.)

We are commanded to have faith, hope, charity, and love,

with an eye single to the glory of God, for this qualifies us for the work of being good parents, good Christians, good citizens. That is what is expected of both fathers and mothers.

If we have any faith at all in God, if we recognize our true relationship to him, we cannot escape the responsibility he has placed upon us.

A bad and neglectful parent cannot lay claim to Christian virtues; a good parent is among the noblest works of God.

A FATHER'S OBJECTIVE

The objective of every father on earth should be to emulate the example of our Father in Heaven as far as that is possible in mortal life.

Christ is our example for righteous living, of course, but so is His Eternal Father — and ours. The ministry of the Father and the Son are the same, both laboring together in complete unity.

Jesus taught us often about our Father. He made it clear beyond any doubt that His Father is also our Father when He said to Mary after the resurrection:

"Go to my brethren, and say unto them, I ascend unto my Father, and your Father; and to my God, and your God." (John 20:17.)

We are the offspring of God as Paul said (Acts 17:28-29), and the whole purpose of our life is to become like Him. That is why the Savior commanded: "Be ye therefore perfect, even as your Father which is in heaven is perfect." (Matt.5:48.)

So we must emulate Him, remembering at all times that He is our Father and can teach earthly fathers about fatherhood in a perfect way. His objectives therefore should be the goals of all earthly fathers.

And what are these goals? "To bring to pass the immortality and eternal life of man." (Moses 1:39.)

Then the objective of every earthly father should be to bring about the eternal life of each member in his own family. And what qualifies him for such a task?

In the Lord's own words: "Faith, virtue, knowledge, temperance, patience, brotherly kindness, godliness, charity, humility, diligence." (D&C 4:6.)

He also said: "Faith, hope, charity and love, with an eye single to the glory of God, qualify him for work." (D&C 4:5.)

There we have it. Men who believe in the revelations of God must certainly give close heed to these words. In the first place, the law to become like God is itself a firm commandment. Since the traits of divine character are outlined so clearly, we cannot mistake our responsibility as fathers.

Kindness, love, patience and godliness must all begin with the manner in which father treats his wife, the mother of the family. Any cruelty toward her, any lack of consideration, becomes a violation of the charter which God has given to fathers.

He commands men most firmly to love and cherish their wives (D&C 42:22) and when that is accomplished, the parental love extends to the children, forming a family circle of loyalty, harmony and righteousness.

As we read the Sermon on the Mount, we see many direct instructions pertaining to the objectives of the Father. Purity of heart is one; being peacemakers is another; holding before others an example of good works is still another. A willingness to be forgiving, and even to pray for our enemies is also commanded. (Matt. 5:45, 6:14-15.)

Forgiveness is so important, for if we fail in this, we jeopardize the forgiveness we hope to receive ourselves.

How can fathers and mothers implement all of these things in the family and thus properly rear their children? Simply by living the gospel in the home, and making it our formula of life. Is there any other way?

HONOR THY MOTHER

There are many conflicting philosophies in the world, and one of them has to do with having children.

Some nations, like Japan, the United States and some European countries foster birth control and even penalize families that have more than two children.

On the other hand there are countries that feel the need for increased population, and in these instances, mothers are rewarded for having large families.

Russia is one of the nations encouraging more births. Here is what the nation does:

Special awards are given to mothers in each of several classifications, according to the number of children they bear. For all mothers who have ten or more children, the Mother Heroine Order award is granted. For women having seven, eight or nine children, the Order of Motherhood Glory is awarded, and for those with either five or six children the Medal of Motherhood is granted.

Since this program started, 240,000 Russian women have received the top award and 4.1 million have received the second.

According to the Population Reference Bureau here in the USA, American births are fifteen per thousand of population; for the world at large twenty-nine per thousand; and for West Germany, the lowest on the list, ten per thousand of population.

Soviet mothers are given cash awards on the birth of their third and each subsequent child and a monthly allowance with the birth of the fourth and each subsequent child.

Russian women, of course, work at regular occupations just as do their husbands. Under Russian law, women with five or more children can retire on a pension five years earlier than they would normally — at fifty instead of fifty-five.

In Russia the state rears the children and does with them as they please under Communist rule. The women procreate; the government provides "parental" care.

With this, of course, people in the free nations could never agree. There is nothing like home training from father and mother to develop a strong generation.

It is most unfortunate when free nations, in which parents can control and teach their little ones within the sanctuary of the home, deliberately reduce their birth rate. In doing so, they weaken the whole structure of freedom.

Sooner or later they will reap the whirlwind as they allow Communism to steadily reduce the free nations to more and more of a minority.

Russia runs short of food, but she encourages motherhood. We have tremendous surpluses, but we devise even the ugliest methods of reducing our population. Starvation is certainly no problem here, as has been alleged.

Which nation — USA or USSR — is on a sound foundation with respect to family life? Shall we say neither? Both are at fault, one in restricting families, the other in having the state rear its children.

Why should America, of all peoples, with its tremendous surpluses, limit its births? Families are the strength of the nation. As we weaken them, we sow the seeds of our own destruction.

THE PLACE OF WOMEN

Where is woman's place in the world? Her true and proper place?

This is debated worldwide just now, with many extreme notions being foisted upon us, but with cooler heads beginning to take control.

Where is woman's place in the world? It is just where the Lord placed it: at the side of her husband.

And where is man's place in the world? It is by the side of his wife.

And where are their places jointly and cooperatively?

In the home, in the Church, on the farm, often in business or in school, but especially and always — *in the family.*

Family life was prescribed by the Lord from the beginning. It is based on proper marriage, which is ordained of God, and *required* by the Lord for the advancement of both man and woman.

The idea that marriage is outmoded is as devil-inspired as that which invites free love and promiscuity. Physical love is for marriage and marriage alone, and anything less than that is debauching and degrading both to man and woman.

Every child has the right to be well born, but that is possible only under proper marriage arrangements, and in a home which will instill in the child the high ideals of good character, faith in God, and devotion to the general well being.

The Church of Jesus Christ of Latter-day Saints has sponsored the advancement of women from its very outset. It was the Prophet Joseph Smith who set forth the ideals for womanhood. He advocated liberty for women in the purest sense of that word and he gave them liberty to fully express themselves — as mothers, as nurses for the sick, as proponents of high community ideals, and as protectors of good morals.

What more can any woman want for herself? What more could any man want for his wife? What more could any man want than to match that standard in his own conduct?

The Prophet Joseph gave us the Relief Society organization to advance these high purposes for Latter-day Saint women. That society today is a worldwide movement, holding membership in national and world organizations for the advancement of women.

It does not indulge in any of the extreme notions which some adopt. It is a wisely governed organization, presided over by the women themselves. And it is spiritual in its deepest concept.

It teaches faith in God and affirms that the glory of God is intelligence. Hence it promotes intelligence, education, high ideals of conduct and the building of strong homes and families.

Every Latter-day Saint woman should be a member of that society, should accept its program, and benefit thereby. Every man should encourage his wife and daughters to become affiliated with it. It is a mighty organization for the good of women themselves, but also for the blessing of families and whole communities.

THAT SECOND SALARY

If you are a young mother and are considering going out to work — leaving your children with others — are you sure it will be a good thing?

Many women seek employment thinking to upgrade the family's standard of living. Many others, of course, work out of sheer necessity.

But what of the working mother who really doesn't have to be the breadwinner, but who merely seeks "self expression" or an escape from the routine of home and children? Does the extra job really pay?

Parents magazine, in a recent issue, raised these questions. It listed many expenses directly associated with the mother leaving the children and going out to work. It mentioned such things as cost of transportation, lunches, babysitters, additional clothes, union or professional dues, insurance, pension plans, office contributions, lunch breaks, and other "inevitable and unexpected dollar dribbles," and then said:

"Now subtract these total costs from your take-home pay, that is, from your net after the employer has made his deductions for taxes, Social Security and disability insurance. What's left is what you're actually going to earn. Is it worth it? Or would your family be better off economically and socially if you stayed home and helped the children?"

The article then goes on to say: "Staying home may turn out to make more economic sense."

The magazine then suggests that the young mother might well stay with the children and do her motherly job, and while the children are sleeping, or in evenings, take up some studies which might lead to a better work position when circumstances permit.

It says that planning like this might make it possible for the woman, when she finally does begin to work, to start as a dental hygienist instead of a file clerk, or a management supervisor instead of an assembly line hand, as examples.

But be that as it may. What should be the main consideration of the mother? It should be the welfare, care and training of the children!

Who can compare good character in a child with a few hundred dollars a month? Who can compare a child's faith in God with whatever gains a young mother may find in clerking for a store or working on an assembly line?

The primary job of mothers is to "mother," which means to rear and train and teach their children to be good citizens, honest and upright, and above all to believe in and serve Almighty God.

What doth it profit if a mother should gain a salary, if she should lose the divine soul of her child?

MOTHERS AND FAMILIES

Good mothers are heaven-sent. So are good fathers. And good mothers and fathers establish good families. Why not make Mother's Day and Father's Day both Family Days?

Today when family life is being challenged, the sad condition emphasizes more than ever the absolutely essential nature of the family as an institution of civilization, as the foundation of nations, and as the gateway to exaltation in heaven.

Families — if they are based on righteousness — are within the divine plan. They are a must, regarded from every standpoint.

But good families rest upon good parenthood, and that can be found only where righteousness reigns, where proper marriage is honored, and where mothers are fully recognized as daughters of Almighty God.

The apostle Paul spoke of the family as being founded in heaven, and said:

"I bow my knees unto the Father of our Lord Jesus Christ, of whom the whole family in heaven and earth is named." (Eph. 3:14-15.)

We are the family of God. He provided a pattern in that He decreed family life for us here on earth, under the sacred bonds of holy matrimony.

Those who seek to destroy family life strike against God Himself. They are anti-Christ in their thinking. If only they were willing to learn that good family life is the ultimate in our existence! It is an essential part of our progress in both mortality and eternity, to an astonishing extent!

Of all the institutions on earth that we should honor, family life is that institution. Of all the righteous traditions and of all the holy principles God revealed, we should give it high priority.

We must not have mothers without families.

We must not have fathers without families.

We must not have families without holy matrimony.

The very heart and center of each good home, of each righteous family, is a noble mother, a co-creator with God. Can there be a more sacred calling? Is there any career that can even approach it in importance?

To be the mothers of human beings, who themselves are the spirit children of God; to be privileged to rear their little ones, shaping their minds and their destinies, and teaching them of our Father in Heaven, is a mission which can only be measured in infinitude.

Shall we not honor them? But how may we best do so? By living up to the ideals that are so dear to them, by living righteously and obeying the Lord. That is the dearest prayer of every good mother.

MOTHER'S SACRED ROLE

To understand mothers, one needs some comprehension of God and His purposes, for God made mothers.

It was He who created Eve, our first mother. It was He who gave her in marriage to Adam. It was He who commanded them to rear a family. It was all included in God's work. Family life is part of His design.

When He made man in the creation, He made *mankind*, not just Adam, but Eve also, and commanded them to form a family and have children. It was an extension of God's plan in heaven, now brought to earth.

All human beings are the offspring of God in the spirit. Each is a dual personage, having both a spirit and a physical body. The spirit is that part of mankind which is the offspring of God. It is in His image. The body is the house or tabernacle in which the spirit resides and it is in the image of the spirit.

He made us male and female. When we lived with Him in our pre-existence, we were male and female there also.

And what was the purpose of sex? To perpetuate life, God's kind of life! And it was to be done only within the bounds of holy matrimony — no other way.

It was a sacred part of creation which the Almighty assigned to us that we might serve as His partners in placing life on earth and perpetuating the species — God's species, which we are.

This sacred process required motherhood, and this the Lord provided. It was to be sacred, too, because bringing God's spirit children into the world is a holy mission.

But motherhood is far more than procreation. It is the rearing of children as well, rearing them in the ways of truth. Motherhood, like fatherhood, was intended to include all the high virtues, all the strong traits of character required to mold human life into a Christlike pattern, that someday it would fit again into the heavenly realm.

Then we see motherhood and fatherhood taking part in a most sacred process. God had children in heaven. Parents usher them into mortality. God in heaven provided the means of rearing children. Motherhood, together with fatherhood, carries out His decrees here on earth.

And how is this done? We are to:

Teach children faith in Christ, the Son of the living God.

Teach them repentance.

Teach them about baptism in water and have them receive the ordinance.

Teach them about baptism by the Holy Spirit, and have them receive it.

Teach them to pray.

Teach them to walk uprightly before the Lord.

Teach them to honor their father and their mother.

When children are neglected, what happens to these commandments? Are they neglected too? What about our relationship with God?

Where the home is not a sanctuary, where there are no family prayers, no family home evenings, no companionship, no objective teaching of the gospel, what happens to God's design for proper parenthood?

Mother's Day and Father's Day alike should remind both parents of our true relationship with God and of our eternal obligation to honor our sacred trust and rear our children in the faith.

THE ARMOR OF RIGHTEOUSNESS

THE ARMOR OF GOD

The scripture (D&C 76) says that the devil will declare war against the saints of God, and encompass them round about. This he is now doing.

War it is; war to the death, so far as the devil is concerned. He would destroy us all if he could.

He already encompasses us round about! In what way? With pornography, with liquor and drugs, with temptations to lie and steal and defraud. With self-destruction in the guise of pleasure wherein he would take away our morals and make us think that evil is good.

His wiles reach into the innermost circles of family life. Hence, we must take upon ourselves the full armor of God to combat these wiles.

One of our most important fortifications is a firm and secure family circle. There, parents will build love at home. There, they will teach faith in Almighty God, teach the little ones as well as themselves of Jesus and His ministry, of Joseph Smith and his divine call.

They will tell about the restoration of the gospel and the mission of the Latter-day Saints. They will teach their children and understand themselves what it means to be a Latter-day Saint.

We all must realize that, in fact, we are a people of divine destiny with a mighty mission to fulfill in these last days. We must understand that to fill that mission we must be prepared and literally forearm ourselves for the fray, because Satan will battle us at every step.

Being Latter-day Saints with this divine destiny, we must renew our dedication to the task before us, and observe each covenant we have made with God, for those covenants are sacred promises to carry on His work.

Then we must identify our foes so that we can successfully combat them. Among those enemies are:

— The tendency for children to rebel against their parents and against the discipline of school and community. They must learn to be good citizens and loyal family members.

— Drugs, alcohol and tobacco which are a deadly menace.

— Immorality, which is surrendering to the enemy. Chastity must be protected as life itself. Pornography is of the devil.

— Dishonesty, which destroys good character. To lie or steal or deceive opens the door wide to the enemy.

— Destruction of marriage, which is one of our worst evils. Marriage is sacred, sex is sacred, babies are sacred. God's people must never be guilty of sacrilege in any form. It is deadly.

But fighting these evils is not enough. We have our divine religion. We have been called into the army of God, which is to set up His kingdom on earth in preparation for the second coming of Christ.

We must be loyal soldiers in that army, firm in our purpose, loyal to every command of our Leader, true to home and Church, and unyielding to the enemy.

We must be intelligent about our religion. We must study it, believe it, and live it. No one can be saved in ignorance. No soldier in any army is efficient if he does not understand his assignment. We must be first-class Latter-day Saints, all of us, and constantly wear the armor of God.

WE ARE IN GOD'S ARMY

Every Latter-day Saint is in the army of Almighty God. Hence we must follow the admonition of the apostle Paul:

"Put on the whole armour of God, that ye may be able to stand against the wiles of the devil.

"For we wrestle not against flesh and blood, but against principalities, against powers, against the rulers of the darkness of this world, against spiritual wickedness in high places.

"Wherefore take unto you the whole armour of God, that ye may be able to withstand in the evil day, and having done all, to stand.

"Stand therefore, having your loins girt about with truth, and having on the breastplate of righteousness;

"And your feet shod with the preparation of the gospel of peace;

"Above all, taking the shield of faith, where with ye shall be able to quench all the fiery darts of the wicked.

"And take the helmet of salvation, and the sword of the Spirit, which is the word of God:

"Praying always with all prayer and supplication in the Spirit, and watching thereunto with all perseverence and supplication for all saints." (Eph. 6:11-18.)

When our work is over, let us then be able to say further with Paul:

"I have fought a good fight, I have finished my course, I have kept the faith:

"Henceforth there is laid up for me a crown of righteousness, which the Lord, the righteous judge, shall give me at that day." (2 Tim. 4:7-8.)

THE SERMON ON THE MOUNT

The Savior's Sermon on the Mount is one of the choicest things in all literature. But not only is it great literature, it is the greatest sermon of which we have record.

What is its primary objective? Is it not to teach people how to get along well with each other, how to improve their habits and build greater characters, how to become Christlike?

Read this sermon regularly, and it will make you a greater and better soul. It is uplifting in every respect, it establishes proper standards of conduct, it points to human frailties and offers a remedy.

Consider just a few of its precepts:

Seek a reconciliation with anyone whom you have offended.

Love your friends, but also your enemies and pray for them.

Ye are the salt of the earth — do not lose the savor.

Ye are a light to the world — let your light shine before men that they may see your good example and hopefully follow it.

Forgive men their trespasses as you hope to be forgiven of God.

Lay up treasures in heaven.

In all your priorities, seek first the kingdom of God.

Don't be a hypocrite, nor try to serve opposing causes.

And then there is the Lord's Prayer. Is anything more sublime? And the Beatitudes!

The meek, the pure in heart, those that mourn, those who hunger and thirst after righteousness, the merciful, the persecuted, the peacemakers — all are blessed.

For a steady source of direction and inspiration, read some of it every day — and all of it once a month. It is priceless!

IN OUR STRIDE

So many unusual things are happening these days that some people no longer seem surprised at anything. At least that is their claim.

"We just take them in our stride. What will be will be," is their fatalistic philosophy.

It may be wonderful to take frightful disasters "in our

stride," but if we do so are we intelligent about it? Can we ignore them and their meaning as we take them in our stride? Do these occurrences have some special significance?

A series of most unusual events happened within the past few weeks. Of course the most startling was the Mount St. Helens eruption, with all its damage and toll of human life.

But while it was belching forth, a series of tornadoes swept through the middle section of the United States. More than nine hundred "freak" storms struck America within that month. In a single day fifty tornadoes were counted in six states. The very next day twenty-four more tornadoes struck Iowa and Nebraska. And during this same period earthquakes shook California.

Have we forgotten the floods in Arizona and Louisiana? Can anyone take them in their stride and ignore them? Certainly those who were caught up in them will not forget them very soon, nor will they recover from them in a hurry.

These natural disasters were killers. They destroyed millions of dollars worth of property. Many people lost all they possessed, all they had worked for during their entire lifetime. Who can take that in their stride? And what of those who were killed?

It is important that we look for significance in these upheavals. Can it be that they are signs of the times? Can it be that the Lord is speaking to America by these frightful disasters?

He said that in the latter days He would declare His testimony by means of tempests, floods, earthquakes and epidemics. He didn't mention volcanoes, but surely they are within His realm as much as earthquakes. Did He force Mount St. Helens into eruption as a warning to Americans to repent and recognize Him?

We have a tendency to forget our pains quickly, even as does a mother when her child is born. Little is said even now about the Arizona floods, although the debris and broken bridges remain.

Even the volcano is off the front pages. And the fifty tornadoes in one day? They got only two inches of space on the front page as part of a news summary. Not so much as a headline was given them!

It is possible to become so hardened that we brush aside the warning voice, and even forget our sufferings. Those who lost their homes and loved ones won't easily forget, though, even if the general public does.

Must the Lord speak in louder tones? Must He send greater disasters before we listen to His warning voice?

How much does it take to waken us to a realization that God is real, that there is an end to His patience, and that the only true security in these troubled times is through obedience to the Most High? Why fly in the face of Providence?

A PEOPLE OF DESTINY

President David O. McKay used to teach the Latter-day Saints in these words:

"Remember who you are and act accordingly."

We are indebted to his great counselor, President N. Eldon Tanner, for reminding us frequently of that wise counsel.

Who are we, that we may know how to act appropriately?

The Latter-day Saints are a people of destiny! This some may not recognize, but this we are in fact. A people of destiny: What is meant by that?

The prophet Daniel spoke of a kingdom to be built up in latter days which eventually would fill the whole earth. It would be a divinely planned and established kingdom. It would be as a stone cut from the mountains without hands. It would establish a righteous regime and stand forever. (Dan. 2:31-45.)

The scriptures speak often of the millennial reign of the Savior to take place in the latter days. However, it was to be preceded by the prior establishment of His kingdom which would prepare the way for the Savior's rule on earth.

It would be a fulfillment of the request in the Lord's Prayer:

"Thy kingdom come. Thy will be done in earth, as it is in heaven." (Matt. 6:10.)

How was that kingdom to be established on earth, and was it not set up during the earthly mission of the Lord?

The Savior did establish His Church during His mortal ministry, but there came a falling away and the kingdom was lost among men through apostasy. It would have to be restored in the latter days, otherwise it could not prepare the way for the millennial reign.

How would it be restored? Through the ministry of an angel who would bring the gospel back to earth in the hour of God's judgment, that it might be taken to all nations, kindreds and peoples. (Rev. 14:6-7.)

To whom would it be given? The prophet Amos declared that God only ministers through His prophets. (Amos 3:7.) God would have to raise up a new prophet since there were none in the apostate world. This He did in the person of the Prophet Joseph Smith, Jr. early in the nineteenth century.

Through that Prophet the divine kingdom was again established on earth. Of this, the Lord Himself said as He spoke to the early workers in this last dispensation: "Wherefore, gird up your loins and be prepared. Behold, the kingdom is yours, and the enemy shall not overcome." (D&C 38:9.)

That kingdom is The Church of Jesus Christ of Latter-day Saints which was organized under the direction of Almighty God by the Prophet Joseph Smith in western New York on April 6, 1830.

And its purpose was to prepare the way. Said he: "Wherefore, gird up your loins and I will suddenly come to my temple." (D&C 36:8.)

As He so spoke, He identified Himself as the Lord Jesus Christ. It is He who will come. It is He who will reign during that millennium. But His "little flock," as He spoke of it in early Church history, must begin to prepare the way. "Fear not, little flock," He said, "the kingdom is yours until I come." (D&C 35:27.)

They must prepare the way. They must become a people of destiny, and as Daniel said, eventually this kingdom will fill the whole earth.

The Church of Jesus Christ of Latter-day Saints is that kingdom. It is for all who will believe. It will continue to grow into its ultimate fruition and we, its members, are the people of destiny who must carry it on. Hence we must remember who we are, and act accordingly.

OUR WORD OF HONOR

Honor is becoming more and more of a scarce "commodity" among men these days. It is indeed ironic that some firms must advertise that they are honest, and that they "care," whatever that means in today's parlance.

An honest man may be the noblest work of God, but honesty is being challenged now from the cradle to the grave — from the facilities at birth to the facilities in the burial, and in many places in between.

Dishonesty seems to be a way of life with many people, and to take advantage of others is regarded by many as the smart thing to do. How far down the hill of character we have fallen!

How refreshing it is, though, when honest acts are seen, and when honest people are found. What a sobering thing, in these days, that editors regard it as news when a boy will find a wallet and return it. Can honesty be so scarce?

One of the great men of the Church was Dr. Karl G. Maeser, our pioneer educator. Speaking of honor at one time he said:

"I have been asked what I mean by word of honor. I will tell you. Place me behind prison walls — walls of stone ever so high, ever so thick, reaching ever so far into the ground. There is a possibility that in some way or another I may be able to escape.

But stand me on the floor and draw a chalk line around me and have me give my word of honor never to cross it. Can I get out of that circle? No, never! I would die first."

If only every one of us could be like Dr. Maeser!

OUR STAND FOR LIBERTY

The gospel of Jesus Christ is our greatest expression of genuine freedom.

In it, free agency is provided. Without it we would all be slaves. Powers in the world that take away the right of free agency, freedom of speech, press, worship and assembly, contribute to such slavery.

Every person who believes in Christ should be staunch in standing for his individual and political liberty. The Book of Mormon teaches us that the Spirit of God is also the Spirit of Freedom. (Alma 61:15.)

The Epistle of James speaks of the gospel as the perfect law of liberty (James 1:25). Paul repeatedly spoke of the liberty we have in the gospel. (Rom. 8:21; Gal. 5:1.) The Savior said of the gospel, "And ye shall know the truth, and the truth shall make you free." (John 8:32.)

It is part of the religion of the Latter-day Saints to believe in liberty and to fight for it and defend it as necessary.

At no time should we in any way compromise our position to those who seek to destroy liberty, either in our nation, in our families, or in our personal lives.

There is no salvation in the kingdom of God without free agency.

There is no such thing as slavery in the Lord's house.

Free agency is part of divinity. Without it there is no progress, intellectually, spiritually, or even physically.

IT IS A WAY OF LIFE

Why is the gospel a way of life? Is it not that the gospel actually is a pattern of the Christlike way, designed to help us become like God?

Most people in the world have no idea as to the real purpose of existence. They do not know why they are even alive. They do not know what comes after mortality, if anything. They are as flotsam on the sea of life.

The restoration of the gospel has given us the answers. Through it we know for a certainty that there is a God in heaven, and furthermore that He is actually our Father.

That is why Jesus taught us to pray: "Our Father which art in heaven, Hallowed be thy name." (Matt. 6:9.) That is why Paul taught that we are God's offspring. (Acts 17:28.)

Especially are we taught that since God is our Father, it is altogether possible — indeed it is expected and commanded — that we become like Him. (Matt. 5:48.)

That is our identity. That is our destiny. We are the children of God. We can become like Him, and He has given us the pattern to follow by which we may actually become like Him.

That pattern is the gospel. That is why the gospel is a way of life. That is why we must follow it day by day. We cannot achieve perfection — like unto God — by imperfect means.

THE BATTLE IS CRITICAL

The Lord indicated that in the last days conditions would arise similar to those in the days of Noah.

In that day there was nearly every form of vice. Dishonesty

obviously was all about; mockery of all things spiritual and rampant unchastity were the rule of the day.

Sodom and Gomorrah appear subsequently in scripture to be an isolated case where the Lord could no longer stand the stench of such sin, but the case was far from being exceptional.

Anyone reading of the moral conditions in Canaan before the coming of the Israelites knows that corruption was everywhere present. So it was in the time of Noah. And so it was with the ancient Greeks and Romans.

So it was still in the days of Peter and Paul. Could we have a more vigorous denunciation of immorality than Paul wrote in some of his epistles?

And so it is with us today. Dishonesty has become almost a way of life with millions of people. Even some in high places in government and business have corrupted themselves through graft and embezzlement.

But the worst onslaught of all is in the realm of morals. Without going into sordid details, what should Latter-day Saints do in this present day? They have the scriptures, describing the conditions of the past. They have the predictions for the future, and they have the commandments in which they are shown the true way of life.

Shall Latter-day Saints yield to these awful temptations? Shall their children? The Lord said that the devil would declare war against the Saints (D&C 76:29), and he is doing so. Shall we become casualties in this conflict? Shall we yield to the devil? Everyone who tempts us is an emissary of the devil!

The advice in Proverbs (6:20-32) is especially appropriate for today. This we should steadfastly observe. We read there:

"My son, keep thy father's commandment, and forsake not the law of thy mother:

"Bind them continually upon thine heart, and tie them about thy neck.

"When thou goest, it shall lead thee; when thou sleepest, it shall keep thee; and when thou awakest, it shall talk with thee.

"For the commandment is a lamp; and the law is light; and reproofs of instruction are the way of life:

"To keep thee from the evil woman, from the flattery of the tongue of a strange woman.

"Lust not after her beauty in thine heart; neither let her take thee with her eyelids.

"For by means of a whorish woman a man is brought to a piece of bread: and the adulteress will hunt for the precious life.

"Can a man take fire in his bosom, and his clothes not be burned?

"Can one go upon hot coals, and his feet not be burned? . . .

"But whoso committeth adultery with a woman lacketh understanding: he that doeth it destroyeth his own soul."

The advice is no different for a woman. She too will destroy her own soul if she should yield to an evil man. There are not two standards in the eyes of the Lord.

As Latter-day Saints we must teach and speak and live virtue all the days of our lives, keeping our minds as well as our bodies clean.

YOU CAN'T TAKE IT?

"You can't take it with you" is an expression used so often with regard to our wealth and worldly possessions here on earth. And of course we don't expect to take any of that with us as we depart this life, much as some would like to.

But there is something we can — and do — take with us, and it is more important than all the gold and property we might amass in our lifetime. What we do take with us is our character, and that character is so important that our entire future existence — in fact all eternity — will be affected by it.

Our character. That is what will be judged at the last day.

That is what will determine whether we will go to a telestial, terrestrial, or celestial glory. And to attain the highest degree, that character must be Christlike.

If we hope to go with Him in the world to come, we must first become like Him, just as He said. Of the Nephites He asked the question: "What manner of men ought ye to be?" Then He Himself gave the answer: "Even as I am." (3 Ne. 27:27.)

Scripture teaches repeatedly that no unclean thing may come into His presence. It likewise sets forth the things that God hates, such as pride, deception and "an heart that deviseth wicked imaginations, feet that be swift in running to mischief, a false witness that speaketh lies, and he that soweth discord among brethren" (Prov. 6:18-19).

Much is said also about virtue and its effect upon good character, and how its violation corrodes our souls. Honesty is a basic tenet of our faith. Dishonesty breaks down character almost as rapidly as does immorality; the two are twin evils; they often go hand in hand.

The eighteenth chapter of Ezekiel provides a clear explanation of how we take our character with us, and what it does to us as we stand before the judgment bar of God.

As that prophet explains, if we overcome our evil tendencies and for the rest of our lives "keep my statutes and do that which is lawful and right. . . . all his transgressions that he hath done shall not be mentioned unto him. In his righteousness that he hath done he shall live."

"But," says the prophet, "when the righteous turneth away from his righteousness and committeth iniquity, and doeth according to all the abominations that the wicked man doeth, shall he live?

"All his righteousness that he hath done shall not be mentioned; in his trespass that he has trespassed and in his sin that he hath sinned, in them shall he die."

It seems that the final judgment will rest largely upon the kind of character we have developed by the time we die. It is that which we take with us.

It is understandable, then, why the Savior spoke of laying up "treasures in heaven, where neither moth nor rust doth corrupt."

OUR WAY OF LIFE

God has said that His ways are not man's ways, and every true follower of Christ should recognize this.

It was He who gave us the pattern by which we should shape our lives here on earth. His life is that pattern. His laws and commandments are the specifications of that pattern.

When He taught us that although we are in the world, we must not be of the world, He meant just that. And why? Why is He so insistent on our keeping His commandments?

It comes back to that oft-repeated, but little understood, scripture found in the Sermon on the Mount: "Be ye therefore perfect, even as your Father which is in heaven is perfect." (Matt. 5:48.)

There is no greater expression in all holy writ. Those few words teach us a great lesson: We are the children of God and our purpose in life is to become like Him.

How many people on earth know the purpose of life? How many theorize and grope through the dark, not knowing why they are here, whence they came, or whither they are bound?

By revelation and through the holy scriptures, we know the answers. Isn't it exhilarating to understand that we are the offspring of Almightly God? Isn't it stimulating to realize that as such, we can become like Him? What a destiny! What a purpose!

But there is a pattern to follow in achieving this great objective. Man's ways will not do. Only God's ways. The gospel is the plan. His Church is the means by which we develop this perfection, and obedience to His laws will alone bear the fruits of success.

To receive His commandments with a doubtful heart, or to keep them with slothfulness, will bring condemnation upon our heads. (D&C 58:26-29.)

Only an enthusiastic response will do, for we are to serve Him with whole heart, might, mind and strength. It will require our all to achieve this divine destiny. That must be our way of life.

THE LORD IS STRICT

The Lord is infinite, being divine as He is. And since He is infinite He is infinite in all of His attributes.

He is infinitely powerful, so we speak of Him as being omnipotent. He is infinitely wise, so we speak of Him as being omniscient. His Holy Spirit by which He controls all things is everywhere present. Hence we speak of Him as being omnipresent.

But He is infinitely merciful too, and loving, and kind. He is infinitely helpful, and His great work is to help us to become like Him. And what greater kindness could there be than that?

But the Lord also is just and He is strict. He cannot look upon sin with the least degree of allowance. No unclean thing may enter His presence. And yet our destiny is to come before Him, live with Him, and become perfect, as He is.

But we achieve our destiny only upon the true laws of progress, which are the principles of the gospel. If we obey, we achieve. If we do not, we fail.

One of the basic rules of the Lord is that we cannot become perfect by imperfect means, by half-hearted obedience, by compromising righteousness. We must be wholehearted, or we fail.

That is why the Lord said: "O ye that embark in the service of God, see that ye serve him with all your heart, might, mind and strength, that ye may stand blameless before God at the last day." (D&C 4:2.)

That is what He means, literally. His first and great command is the same, in slightly different language, but again it demands that we love Him with all our hearts and souls. (Matt. 22:38.)

Here is where the Lord is strict. Halfway measures will do little good. Passive membership in the Church does not save. We must be anxiously engaged in the service (D&C 58:26-29); we must learn our duty and fulfill it diligently (D&C 107:99-100).

And we must endure to the end. The Savior said: "Whoso taketh upon him my name, and endureth to the end, the same shall be saved." (3 Ne. 27:6.) But He said further: "He that endureth not unto the end, the same is he that is also hewn down and cast into the fire, from whence they can no more return." (3 Ne. 27:17.)

The Lord made it clear that only those who are valiant in the testimony of Jesus shall enter His presence (D&C 76:78-79.) Being valiant is certainly being anxiously engaged, being diligent in keeping the commandments, and serving Him with all our heart, might, mind and strength.

Each one may easily enough determine if he himself is valiant by simply measuring his obedience to the strict rules the Lord has provided for exaltation.

BE RECONCILED

The quality of our worship of the Lord is measured in large degree by our attitude toward our fellowmen.

It was not said lightly by the Lord that the second great

commandment — to love our neighbor as ourselves — was "like unto" the first, to love the Lord our God with all our heart and soul.

Neither was it lightly said that on these two commandments "hang all the law and the prophets" (Matt. 22:40). Could He more clearly have said that all religion is based upon these great laws?

He expects that we will obey these laws. Otherwise He never would have given them.

The Lord taught us how to implement the love of neighbor by giving us the Golden Rule, to do to others as we would be done by. But then there was another commandment.

He taught that when we have difficulty between neighbors, we should seek a reconciliation, and that it should be sought "before we bring our gift to the altar."

He said this: "If thou bring thy gift to the altar, and there rememberest that thy brother hath ought against thee; Leave there thy gift before the altar, and go thy way; first be reconciled to thy brother, and then come and offer thy gift" (Matt. 5:23-24).

It is interesting that in Old Testament days, also, this law was made a special provision of repentance. In two different places Ezekiel, for example, explains that if the individual "hath restored to the debtor his pledge" and "if the wicked restore the pledge, give again that he had robbed" (Ezek. 18:7; 33:15), then forgiveness might come.

But it seems to have been more than just forgiveness when the Savior spoke of it in the Sermon on the Mount. He was talking about worship, and indicated that worship was not acceptable from a sinner until he had accomplished a reconciliation with the injured party.

Without such reconciliation would worship be accepted? Would it be hypocritical? Could we come to the Lord with a broken heart and a contrite spirit, as He requires, if we had ill feelings toward others, or if we had done someone else an injustice and had not made proper adjustment?

Can we have sincere faith without genuine repentance?

Can we have real repentance without the reconciliation of which the Lord speaks? And can we worship properly if we have not repented of our failings?

There is the matter of forgiveness, also, for He has said that "if ye forgive men their trespasses, your heavenly Father will also forgive you: But if ye forgive not men their trespasses, neither will your Father forgive your trespasses" (Matt. 6:14-15).

And if we refuse to take the necessary steps to obtain forgiveness, will our worship be acceptable to the Lord?

ON THE SAFE SIDE

When the Savior ministered among the Nephites, He taught them this important lesson:

"Verily, verily I say unto you, ye must watch and pray always lest ye enter into temptation, for Satan desireth to have you that he may sift you as wheat." (3 Ne. 18:18.)

And when Paul wrote to the Thessalonians concerning the great apostasy and the reign of wickedness on the earth, he said that the evil one will oppose and exalt himself above all that is called God or is worshipped. He said the devil will work with "all power, and signs and lying wonders, and with all deceivableness of unrighteousness."

The result will be that many will revel in sin, and will be led by a "strong delusion that they should believe a lie," and that all who find pleasure in unrighteousness will be damned. (2 Thes. 2:1-12.)

We have been told in the scripture that in the last days, preceding Christ's return, conditions will be as they were in the days of Noah; and hence at His appearance destruction will come upon the wicked as in Noah's day, but not this time by water, rather by fire. (Matt. 24 and Isa. 24.)

The earth will be defiled by widespread sin, "therefore the inhabitants of the earth are burned, and few men left," as Isaiah said.

It was also predicted that there will be a complete separation between the wicked and the righteous, and that the righteous will be protected, even with fire from heaven if that becomes necessary. (D&C 63:54; 1 Ne. 22.)

The separation of the righteous from the wicked must of course be a voluntary act on the part of the righteous, who must not and will not take part in the sins of mankind. They must live their religion, worshipping the Christ, despite all the pressures of the world.

In other words, we must not be of the world, although we live in the world.

Worldliness increases by the day, by the hour. It is beyond even the imagination of the righteous. The increase of crime, the avalanche of deceit and dishonesty, the vast spread of immorality, all reveal the advance of wickedness.

Who, for example, would have thought that, as the *Sacramento Bee* says, one in every six people in San Francisco is homosexual? It is estimated by that newspaper (Dec. 4, 1977) that in that one city alone there are about 150,000 such people and that there are eighteen million of them in America.

The righteous must recognize that there is to be a separation of the followers of the Lord from the wicked. They cannot — and must not — partake of the sins of Babylon, lest they also partake of her plagues.

They must recognize too that only they themselves can bring about this separation. The Lord will not take away their free agency. The believers must exercise it — and choose the right.

As President George Albert Smith used to say so often: Stay on the Lord's side of the line! That becomes the point of separation.